THE 21ST CENTURY SCHOOL LIBRARY

A MODEL FOR INNOVATIVE TEACHING & LEARNING

RYAN BANI TAHMASEB

First published 2021

by John Catt Educational Ltd

15 Riduna Park, Station Road,
Melton, Woodbridge IP12 1QT
UK
Tel: +44 (0) 1394 389850

4500 140th Ave North,
Suite 101, Clearwater,
FL 33762-3848
US
Tel: +1 561 448 1987

Email: enquiries@johncatt.com
Website: www.johncatt.com

ISBN: 978 1 913622 82 4

Set and designed by John Catt Educational Limited

To Katie,
whose love and support never waver,
and to Noah and Grace,
who delight and teach me every day.

Endorsements

Twenty-first century school librarians are leading their school districts in many influential ways. Their efforts in design thinking, inclusivity, anti-racism, teaching multiple literacies, modeling lessons, and collaborative methods are just some of the core leadership efforts that can help transform any school district. Packed with specific examples of how successful school librarians have led from their libraries, *The 21st Century School Library* is a must-read for teachers, administrators, and school librarians who need concrete evidence on how they can develop efficacious school libraries for their school district.

Dr. Krista Welz, school librarian in New Jersey, 2017 recipient of a Library Journal Movers and Shakers award, AASL Social Media Superstar, and co-founder of Edcamp Urban

The 21st Century School Library shows how great instruction benefits students and why empowering the school librarian to lead the way makes for great learning. Bringing in his own experiences and sharing the great thinking of librarians from across the country, Ryan Bani Tahmaseb paints a picture of what an essential school librarian looks like. This book is for every librarian who wants to give their students the best library program while working side by side with supportive administrators and teachers. It is perfect for new librarians, experienced librarians, and every colleague they work with.

Tom Bober, author of Building News Literacy: Lessons for Teaching Critical Thinking Skills in Elementary and Middle Schools

In *The 21st Century School Library*, Ryan Bani Tahmaseb takes a deep dive into the role of school librarian. This book is a call to action for schools to utilize their libraries and librarians to help democratize education and allow students to follow their innate intellectual curiosity. Throughout the book, Tahmaseb advocates for student access, genuine inquiry, and opportunities to address real-world problems. He outlines a holistic approach to integrating multiple literacies into classrooms, including racial literacy, and teaching alongside students and teachers in an all-inclusive community — all while exploring collaboration, authentic research, and hands-on learning in a global learning community. This is a must-read for librarians as well as teachers and administrators, as Tahmaseb directly addresses these audiences in each chapter. You will leave this book with a plethora of ideas for making your school library the hub of your school: a place where curiosity, voice, and choice foster learning that is meaningful, inclusive, and engaging for all students.

Tomasen Carey, senior lecturer at the University of New Hampshire and field coordinator for Learning Through Teaching

In a time when school librarians are disappearing from schools, Ryan Bani Tahmaseb presents readers with a timely, relevant, and important look at one of education's most invaluable assets. This book is a useful guide for those of us leading change within school libraries and the colleagues we partner with each day. *The 21st Century School Library* is the perfect blend of theory and practice!

Dr. Kristen Mattson, author of Ethics in a Digital World: Guiding Students Through Society's Biggest Questions

Contents

Foreword

The school library is the heart of the school. It is essential in its location, access, and offerings to support learner-centered classrooms where students are constructing knowledge, designing, thinking, and collaborating. Where else in the school can you find a quiet spot to sit and read a book that allows you to travel to other worlds, meet new friends, or enter another dimension? Libraries are communities for book lovers, provide access to reliable research and information, and even transform into STEM labs and makerspaces.

In my first year of teaching, I learned my school librarian was going to be my best friend. We planned lessons together to help my students research, write, and read powerful literature. She had access to a wealth of knowledge that helped my students learn deeply. A class trip to the library was always a sensory adventure. When we studied the Harlem Renaissance and arrived at the library, jazz music was playing and books about artists, writers, and poets of that time period were spread across the tables for my students to peruse. Students wrote poems based on Romare Bearden paintings while listening to jazz in the library that day. Together, my school librarian and I applied to and attended the National Gallery of Art's Summer Institute in Washington, DC for a week, to be immersed in mythology and learn from various experts and teaching artists. As a result of attending the learning institute, we wrote a curriculum together that we co-taught in our school the following years. She is still a close friend and I consider her a mentor who impacted my early years of teaching.

Fast-forward to today (and 18 years later). I am in a different school but the librarian is still my go-to when I am looking for something good to read, developing a new reading and writing unit, or just want to talk. He does lots of book talks, shows my students which databases to access for information for their research reports, and keeps me in the loop about potential award-winning books I must read. When I walk into the library, it is always filled with students doing homework, collaborating, and working on the computers. My school library is a central spot for students, no matter the time of day.

Ryan Bani Tahmaseb brings to the forefront the magic and power of school libraries. He provides a practical approach to elevating the level of learning in your school library, redesigning the space to welcome all students and teachers, and rebranding the library from "the room with the old, dusty, smelly books" to a hub for 21st century learning. A library today is a place where books and technology go hand in hand to empower learners, support creativity, and build critical thinkers.

Forward-thinking librarians are always in the know and piloting projects. Erika Long in Nashville, Tennessee, initiated an inquiry-based learning project for teachers and students in her school. Peter Langella in Hinesburg, Vermont, took the lead in his school to create a faculty book study, as well as a series of talks for the community to address racism and anti-Semitism. These are just two examples in a book that spotlights many models and mentor librarians who have made positive differences in their schools and communities. Ryan shows us that librarians are leaders and change-makers.

Reading *The 21st Century School Library* reminds me that libraries and librarians are crucial in our democratic society. Throughout the book Ryan provides practical ways for librarians to work with teachers to put more books in students' hands that represent the diversity in our nation, bring attention to valid and reliable research and information, support digital citizenship, and gain funding for books, technology and after-school programs, as well as start a makerspace lunch group or after-school STEM club. He has connected his readers with amazing and inspiring librarians around the country who share their own knowledge and expertise. To build a better world we need access to information, knowledge, and ideas so young people are literate in all the facets of literacy. Ryan shows us how librarians and libraries can help pave the way to inspire and motivate knowledgeable and caring lifelong learners.

Michele L. Haiken, author of New Realms for Writing: Inspire Student Expression with Digital Age Formats

Introduction

School libraries stand at the forefront of innovation in education. Yet many teachers and administrators do not know what to make of them, much less how to best utilize their varied and valuable resources.

What if school librarians, whose field of practice has transformed in the past few decades, could show us excellent models for innovative teaching and leadership? What if the vital adaptations that school librarians have made could help other educators evolve? What if the lessons learned in the library could be scaled up to benefit all fields of practice and all students? These are the questions we'll explore together in this book.

Each chapter takes an in-depth look at the paradigm-shifting work that school libraries are doing to advance student learning, professional development, and school-wide engagement. We'll consider how library-led, forward-thinking initiatives can guide all educators — teachers and administrators alike — toward transformative educational practices.

I'll walk you through specific examples of what leading school libraries are doing and provide some practical guidance on how K-12 educators of all stripes, including administrators, can adopt these focus areas into their practice — wherever you fall on the spectrum of experience.

There are countless amazing library-led projects, initiatives, and movements happening everywhere, and this book is my humble attempt to provide both a synthesis and an overview of what I have come to understand to be most important through collaborations, conversations, and my own first-hand experiences.

Of course, not all school librarians do great work. This is true of any profession. But the difference here is that, generally speaking, there's a tendency to undervalue, underfund, and undercut school libraries, always to the detriment of the students and teachers they're supposed to serve.

The library should be the heart of the school. It's my hope that this book will help you understand *how* and *why* this is true.

Here's a breakdown of what you can expect in each chapter.

Chapter 1: Prioritizing hands-on learning that addresses real-world problems

School librarians have found that teaching methods that prioritize hands-on learning and address real-world problems spark more genuine interest and creativity from students and educators alike. Teaching methods such as design thinking, inquiry-based learning, and project-based learning give students reasons to use the research process authentically. And while they're working, students gain a newfound understanding of themselves, their peers, and how the world really works.

Chapter 2: Improving access to books, information, and technology

School librarians are charged with making sure students have equitable access to books, information, and technology. From securing access to educational databases that aid student research to ensuring that relevant books and devices are available for students to borrow, school librarians know how and why democratizing education should be at the forefront of educators' minds. This chapter explores how libraries are improving access to books, information, and technology and explains why all educators should consider doing so in their roles.

Chapter 3: Centering inclusivity

School librarians regularly review the latest literature to build resource collections that reflect diversity in each of the "Big 8" social identifiers: age, ethnicity, race, ability, gender, sexual orientation, religion, and socioeconomic status. Because librarians are up to date, they can be helpful guides in goal-setting for administrators, lesson-designing for teachers, and planning school-wide professional development. This chapter shares specific examples of how school libraries center inclusivity and offers practical tips for how these efforts can be extended throughout the school.

Chapter 4: Promoting and teaching multiple literacies

To meet students' evolving needs, libraries are no longer focused exclusively on textual literacy. Librarians now teach multiple forms of literacy, including visual literacy, information literacy, digital literacy, technological literacy, and racial literacy. With many libraries leading the way, educators are getting creative in how and where these skills are taught. The important part is each school's commitment to teaching these literacies across the content areas to ensure that students have adequate practice in honing these skills, each of which they will need in order to be informed, perceptive, and empowered citizens.

Chapter 5: Building meaningful connections to the outside world

School librarians do not face the same exact boundaries as classroom teachers. Considering this, as well as the fact that we live in an increasingly globalized society, school librarians often look beyond the school walls for student learning opportunities. We want to help students understand their place in what the American Association of School Librarians calls "the global learning community." Drawing on specific library-led examples, this chapter takes a closer look at how all educators can facilitate meaningful connections to the outside world for their students.

Chapter 6: Revitalizing research

For many students the research process is dreadfully boring, mostly because they're not given a chance to explore topics they're interested in or develop their own research questions. But when educators invite students to follow their curiosity and eventually create something original that shows their learning and is shared with others, research becomes an exciting opportunity. Because librarians are expert researchers, we often show teachers and students how to liven up the research process and support them throughout the process. This chapter is a tour of what all this looks like in action.

Chapter 7: Modeling and teaching collaboration

Educators who collaborate with each other often find that doing so leads to a more dynamic learning environment, as well as modeling for their students what collaboration can and should look like. Just as important is explicitly teaching collaboration skills to students — skills that enable them to work effectively and efficiently with other people. Given the nature of librarians' work in schools, we're experts at modeling and teaching collaboration. This chapter examines the specifics of how all educators can collaborate well and the ways in which your school librarian can be a collaborative partner.

By emphasizing both function and results, each chapter illustrates why its particular topic is vital for advancing K-12 education. Throughout the book, my own experiences as a school librarian appear alongside those of other school librarians and library-adjacent educators. Each chapter also includes explanations of how to leverage the school librarian as an ongoing resource and collaborator, along with easy-to-follow recommendations for applying what is learned in the chapter to teaching and school leadership. Finally, each chapter provides guiding questions that educators can ask themselves about how they might effectively apply these ideas to their own practice, in their own unique contexts.

This book is ultimately a survey of 21st century school libraries whose guiding principles also serve as a blueprint for innovation in K-12 education. My hope is that what you read in the pages that follow will help you use your library and your librarian better, and that by the end you'll be convinced that school libraries — and all the educators associated with them — indeed offer a compelling vision for the future of our schools.

Chapter 1

Prioritizing hands-on learning that addresses real-world problems

"Curiosity is underrated"

— Rob Bell

I love being a school librarian. Every day, I have the opportunity to collaborate with students and teachers on a variety of lessons, projects, and units. It's a privilege to participate in — and bear witness to — all sorts of educational adventures. And from my vantage point, there is one style of teaching and learning that stands above the rest.

There are different frameworks for this kind of teaching and learning. But each of them points toward the same pedagogical approach: hands-on learning that addresses real-world problems.

As educators, our *approach* to teaching and learning is arguably where we have the most control of student success. And as an approach, hands-on learning that addresses real-world problems is ideal because whenever and wherever it's happening, students and teachers are energized, challenged, even joyful. You can see their genuine interest in the task(s) at hand. You can see their creativity. Best of all, you can see there's plenty of room for making mistakes and learning from them.

Today's forward-thinking school librarians often utilize this approach to teaching and learning because it's in our wheelhouse. We are charged with educational leadership around student inquiry, collaboration, exploration, and engagement. Indeed, these are some of our "key commitments," as laid out by the American Association of School Librarians (AASL).[1] For school librarians, hands-on learning that addresses real-world problems is both a strength and a mandate. It's what we're called to do.

In this chapter, I'll show you what this pedagogical approach looks like in action, in my own teaching practice and that of other forward-thinking school librarians. I'll explore how our use of this approach can serve as a blueprint for innovation in other areas of teaching and administration in K-12. Then I'll explain how you can leverage the school librarian as an ongoing resource and collaborator for this work, providing easy-to-follow recommendations for applying what is learned to both teaching and school administration.

But first, I'll walk you through three specific — and increasingly popular — frameworks that fall under the umbrella of hands-on learning that addresses real-world problems. This will give us some common language and hopefully help you see their commonalities — that they are all, in essence, driven by the same general philosophy.

Project-based learning

PBLWorks, a nonprofit organization committed to building teacher capacity around project-based learning, defines PBL as "a teaching method in which students learn by actively engaging in real-world and personally meaningful projects."[2]

I like this definition because it stresses the importance of student projects that are "personally meaningful" and rooted in the real world. This feels right. When we give students permission to study a topic that is of personal interest to them — often something that's not directly taught in school — we help them bridge the gap between school and the world

---

1   American Association of School Librarians. (2018) *AASL Standards Framework for Learners*, American Library Association. https://standards.aasl.org/wp-content/uploads/2017/11/AASL-Standards-Framework-for-Learners-pamphlet.pdf

2   www.pblworks.org/what-is-pbl

outside, the so-called real world. In this way, school becomes *part of* the real world, instead of separate from it. This is no small thing.

In their book *Project Based Teaching*, Suzie Boss and John Larmer lay out specific teaching practices for PBL, each of which helps the educator move from "the all-knowing expert who transmits knowledge" to "well-informed coach, facilitator of learning, and guide through the inquiry process."[3] Their seven project-based teaching practices, listed and summarized below, provide a nice overview of what project-based learning looks like from the educator's perspective.

1. **Build the culture.** Shift the focus from yourself to your students, who are given permission to explore topics of interest to them. Create a classroom environment where collaboration is key, risk-taking is encouraged, and plenty of time is provided to work out possible solutions.

2. **Design and plan.** Before beginning a project, gather all the resources your students will need to work effectively and efficiently. Connect with other educators, inside and/or outside your school, to learn from their expertise. You may also enlist them to come in and work with you and your students during the project.

3. **Align to standards.** Make sure you have clearly articulated learning goals and a plan for how project-based learning will help your students achieve them. This is how PBL stays grounded.

4. **Manage activities.** Have in mind specific strategies (routines, calendars, checkpoints, etc.) for helping students work independently and collaboratively, leaving room for students to take risks and make mistakes.

5. **Assess student learning.** Have a plan for assessment that is rooted in student growth and includes feedback from not only you, but also other students and collaborating teachers.

6. **Scaffold student learning.** This is all about equity. Make sure scaffolding resources are available to students who need them; this, of course, requires you to have a good sense of who your students are as learners.

---

3   Boss, S. with Larmer, J. (2018) *Project Based Teaching: How to Create Rigorous and Engaging Learning Experiences*, ASCD

7.   **Engage and coach.** Guide students through the learning process via mini-lessons, soliciting their ideas and feedback throughout the process, demonstrating your high standards, and cheerleading during their successes and their failures.

Given these teaching practices, it's easy to understand why PBL is a framework popular with many educators today. Student inquiry is front and center, which naturally leads to increased student engagement and interest, and often even a reinvigorated or newfound passion for learning.

Design thinking

With origins in engineering and product development, design thinking is increasingly adopted as an educational framework. It's useful within the K-12 world because it's focused on empathy: throughout the design process, students are encouraged to think deeply about what others want and need. Then they work creatively and collaboratively to make some kind of solution or product. Blake Sims St. Louis, program director of social innovation at Boston University, describes design thinking as an "authentic, but often messy, process for exploring and addressing complex, real-world problems."

The "messy" part is important. It's also what holds so many educators back from giving this framework a try — or, for that matter, the others I'm outlining here. The problem is that if we're risk-averse as educators then our students tend to follow suit.

The design thinking framework gives students the time, space, and guidance they need to be creative, in terms of ability to imagine and ability to make. Messiness is a crucial element of creativity. In fact, the mess actually becomes *the means through which* students learn important problem-solving and critical thinking skills.

In *LAUNCH: Using Design Thinking to Boost Creativity and Bring Out the Maker in Every Student*, John Spencer and A.J. Juliani argue that design thinking "isn't a subject, topic, or class. It's more a way of solving problems that encourages positive risk-taking and creativity. And when you start looking for examples of design thinking, you'll see it all over the place."[4]

---

4   Spencer, J. & Juliani, A.J. (2016) *LAUNCH: Using Design Thinking to Boost Creativity and Bring Out the Maker in Every Student*, Dave Burgess Consulting

Depending on where you look, you'll see the design thinking framework, or "way of solving problems," articulated in different terms. The language that I use, shared in the list below, was created through a collaboration between Blake Sims St. Louis and the technology team at my school, led by Jonathan Schmid. We're a Pre-K–8 school, so the terminology is intentionally simple, but it's fairly representative of how other schools articulate this framework.

Before the first step, teachers need to determine learning goals. Next they should decide between selecting a topic for the class to address or allowing the students to select a topic themselves. And then they need to choose whether students will work independently or in groups.

1. **Understand.** To begin the project, provide students with opportunities to read about their topic, ask questions, research, and talk to experts. The goal is to gather as much information as possible that could be used further down the line and, in the process, to develop empathy for the "user" of the "product" they'll eventually make.

2. **Define.** Give students plenty of space and time to reflect on what was learned in the "understand" phase, with the ultimate goal of analyzing trends and identifying exactly what it is that the "user" needs or wants.

3. **Imagine.** This is the brainstorming phase, where ideas should be wild and free. No idea is a bad idea. When all ideas have been listed, you can help students evaluate them. Which ideas offer the best routes forward for addressing the needs or wants of the "user"? Which can most likely be completed in the time allotted?

4. **Prototype.** Students put together their first draft or sketch. Ideally, you'll require them to create something physical that others can interact with in some way. This is when you can bring students into a makerspace, if you have one, or provide simple materials like cardboard and duct tape.

5. **Try.** Provide opportunities for students to gather feedback on their prototype. What's working? What's not? Have students apply this feedback to the process of making a new and improved iteration of their prototype.

As you can see, design thinking involves lots of hands-on experimentation and interaction with other people. Again, its empathy-based approach — the way it centers what is needed by others — is its defining feature. Students come out on the other side with not only a better understanding of themselves as learners, but also the world around them.

Inquiry-based learning

The Center for Inspired Teaching defines inquiry-based learning as "a pedagogical approach that invites students to explore academic content by posing, investigating, and answering questions ... [This] approach puts students' questions at the center of the curriculum, and places just as much value on the component skills of research as it does on knowledge and understanding of content."[5]

The best part of inquiry-based learning is that questions are ultimately more important than answers. So many of our students are answers-focused, because we've taught them to see learning as an impersonal process where they are assigned a task and their job is to provide an answer that satisfies the teacher. But if students are given enough opportunities to pursue questions that are genuinely of interest to them, they become more excited about the learning process and better able to discover answers on their own. When we allow students to pursue self-developed lines of inquiry, we help set them on the path to becoming lifelong learners.

In *Inspiring Curiosity*, Colette Cassinelli, a library instructional technology teacher, explains that a key attribute of inquiry-based learning "is that students' own driving questions propel their research. The spark of curiosity bridges the gap between what they know and do not know. Learners steer the direction of their inquiry as they consider the best way to uncover stories or unexpected ideas."[6] Accordingly, learning becomes not only more exciting to students, but also a form of self-empowerment. They come to understand that they're the captains of their own ships and that their options for learning and exploring are endless.

5   Center for Inspired Teaching. (2008) *Inspired Issue Brief: Inquiry-Based Teaching.* https://inspiredteaching.org/wp-content/uploads/impact-research-briefs-inquiry-based-teaching.pdf

6   Cassinelli, C. (2018) *Inspiring Curiosity: The Librarian's Guide to Inquiry-Based Learning*, International Society for Technology in Education

Before students get started, do what you can to create a classroom environment — or, if you're an administrator, a *school* environment — in which students are regularly encouraged to share their ideas freely and take risks. This kind of environment is incredibly important for inquiry-based learning, because it increases the likelihood that students will trust their own instincts and be willing to share their genuine interests and questions with you and their classmates. Doing this kind of work on the front end of inquiry-based learning pays dividends throughout the entire process.

Heather Wolpert-Gawron, a teacher and PBL coach, argues that you should begin by modeling what the inquiry process looks like. Essentially, you walk students through your own process of inquiry about a topic of great interest to you. When they see your passion about the process, they're much more likely to buy in. In an article for *Edutopia*, Wolpert-Gawron puts it like this: "Inquiry-based learning, if front-loaded well, generates such excitement in students that neurons begin to fire, curiosity is triggered, and they can't wait to become experts in answering their own questions."[7] Once you and your students are excited, you can begin.

Below is a summary of Cassinelli's inquiry-based learning framework.[8]

1. **Curiosity.** Work directly with your students to develop a list of topics of interest related to the subject at hand. What piques their curiosity? What problems related to this subject do they know about? What do they feel emotionally connected to?

2. **Ask questions.** Once students have selected a specific topic, model for them how to ask good questions about it. Give them specific language. Encourage students to develop their own questions about their topics, then help them revise, clarify, and prioritize these questions through individualized feedback.

3. **Investigate.** Help students find and curate the resources they need to answer their questions. Teach (or review) how to research

---

7   Wolpert-Gawron, H. (2016) "What the heck is inquiry-based learning?", *Edutopia*. www.edutopia.org/blog/what-heck-inquiry-based-learning-heather-wolpert-gawron

8   Cassinelli, C. (2018) *Inspiring Curiosity: The Librarian's Guide to Inquiry-Based Learning*, International Society for Technology in Education

effectively, especially how to evaluate online sources for credibility. If possible, help them connect with experts outside school.

4. **Create.** This step essentially involves synthesizing the information gathered into a coherent "answer." Your role becomes guiding students through the process of figuring out how to best communicate their answer. Have them consider their audience. How can the information they've gathered tell a story that caters to their audience? What can they create to tell this story?

5. **Share.** Based on the nature of your students' creations, help them facilitate some kind of authentic sharing experience for those creations. The goal here is to provide a real audience — ideally identified in the previous step — who can observe, appreciate, and provide feedback.

6. **Reflect.** Provide your students with time and space to reflect on what they created and the process that led to its creation. Ask them if they feel their creation successfully answered their question. Why or why not? Give students opportunities to think critically about their learning style.

Inquiry-based learning helps students to trust and follow their innate curiosity about the world. In the process, they learn to ask good questions and become increasingly independent in the research process — important skills that will help them in school and beyond.

Hands-on learning that addresses real-world problems

The three frameworks I've outlined have distinct differences, but they each operate from a similar ideology. In this section I'll discuss some key similarities.

With these frameworks, your role as an educator becomes less of a "sage on the stage" and more of a skilled facilitator and guide. This is a big and important mindset shift. It's big because of its implications for your students' self-sufficiency, and it's important because this kind of learning can help increase student interest and engagement in the learning process.

You're not exactly doing more work or less work; you're doing *different* work. You're preparing mini-lessons to explicitly teach certain skills.

You're showing students how to organize and synthesize the information they gather. You're arranging for experts to visit your classroom or connect with your class virtually. You're collaborating with technology teachers, school librarians, art teachers, or whoever is willing and excited to help your students with whatever it is you're guiding them through.

Your students, however, *are* doing more work. Because they're acting on their own interests and questions, their minds are fully engaged. They have neither time nor reason to be bored or disengaged. They're incredibly, even surprisingly, eager to learn — all because you've given them permission to use their imagination, notice what interests them, pursue their unique or even outlandish ideas, trust their intuition, and, most importantly, *to create*. This is one of the guiding principles behind these frameworks: all students are creative. Educators who employ project-based learning, design thinking, or inquiry-based learning know in their bones that this is true.

Throughout the process, mistakes are welcome, expected, and even encouraged. Risk-taking becomes second nature in this kind of learning. I tell my students that my most valuable educational experiences have come right after I've failed at something, because failure often allows us to look at a problem from different angles — and one of those angles might be the key to a more successful attempt. In fact, this is how we encourage innovation in our classrooms. When we give students space to make mistakes and learn from them, they naturally begin to make attempts that are new and different. According to *The Innovator's Mindset* by George Couros, "new" and "different" are the twin components of innovation.[9]

Each framework also assumes a kind of longer-term project. Students have the opportunity to dive deeply into a particular topic of interest, and in the process they have the important and true-to-life experience of plugging away at something for a while and seeing where it takes them. They learn to organize their thoughts and materials and take control of their own learning.

---

9   Couros, G. (2015) *The Innovator's Mindset: Empower Learning, Unleash Talent, and Lead a Culture of Creativity*, Dave Burgess Consulting

Students also learn how to find good information on their own, which is important across all subject areas. In a day and age when information is plentiful but not necessarily trustworthy, this is huge. You're expanding their understanding of what research entails. For example, when you help a student find an expert on a particular topic and give them permission to contact that person, you help them see this is something that a person can easily do to find information to support their learning and understanding. People are, in fact, sources. Any journalist can confirm this.

In each of these frameworks, learning is hands-on. Students are huddled together working on a prototype. They're interviewing classroom visitors. They're tinkering in a makerspace. They're using technology, books, found materials, sketchbooks, and more.

Perhaps most importantly, your students are able to wrestle with a real problem or real question that they have about the way the world works. At the end, students experience the satisfaction of producing something they worked hard to create. Even if their product is ultimately unfinished — which, of course, often happens in the real world — they are almost always proud of what they've made and know the steps necessary to finish it in their own time, if they're inclined to do so.

This groundedness in the real world is ultimately what makes this approach to learning so effective. It gives students permission to do in school what people do in the world outside — the world we're tasked with preparing them to enter. They see the real-world application because they live it, individually and as a class. You can see why school librarians like myself — whose job it is to bring about student inquiry, collaboration, exploration, and engagement[10] — often employ hands-on learning that addresses real-world problems.

Responding to criticisms

As with any pedagogical approach, the frameworks I've outlined in this chapter are not without their critics. If you're interested in employing

---

10   American Association of School Librarians. (2018) *AASL Standards Framework for Learners*, American Library Association. https://standards.aasl.org/wp-content/uploads/2017/11/AASL-Standards-Framework-for-Learners-pamphlet.pdf

one of the frameworks for the first time, or perhaps diving more deeply into one of them, chances are you'll be on the receiving end of some of these criticisms — especially if the framework is relatively new to your department, division, school, or district. Perhaps you're even skeptical yourself.

Educator criticisms about innovative teaching approaches sometimes come across as curmudgeonly, but I would argue that they're actually quite helpful to consider. They force us to think carefully and critically about what might not work and then plan accordingly.

Here are a few common criticisms related to hands-on learning that addresses real-world problems, along with my responses to each.

- **No explicit teaching of "skills."** This criticism is actually rooted in a misunderstanding of these frameworks. Skills are still explicitly taught, perhaps most effectively in the form of mini-lessons. Indeed, mini-lessons that teach specific skills or concepts should be *baked into* the unit you create for hands-on learning that addresses real-world problems. You need to be thoughtful about how you scaffold knowledge, so your students can be as successful as possible. Accordingly, you can still use formative assessments to evaluate these skills through fairly traditional methods, such as rubrics, quizzes, and even tests. Your summative assessment is the final product that your students work to create. You teach specific skills all along the way and, even better, you help students hone other skills that are important across all disciplines, such as self-advocacy, critical thinking, and problem-solving.

- **Not structured enough.** This is a big one. Some educators see these frameworks as wishy-washy, free-form projects in which the teacher is mostly uninvolved. Cue the chaos, they say. But, again, this criticism comes from a lack of understanding of how hands-on learning that addresses real-world problems is supposed to work. In this case, well, the frameworks exist for a reason. It's crucial that you follow the frameworks and carefully plan how to structure and execute the entire project, including what each class period will look like, the due dates for the various components, and how you'll assess student learning throughout the process. That said, it's definitely a shift in teaching style. As mentioned earlier, the teacher becomes more of a facilitator; if you haven't done this before, or you've done it and it wasn't immediately successful, then it can feel uncomfortable. But once we push past that discomfort and find our groove, we see that we've created highly structured learning environments that are very conducive to student engagement and productivity.

- **Not rigorous enough.** This one is definitely related to the previous two criticisms. There are many educators out there who cling to a very traditional understanding of what a classroom and a teacher-student relationship are supposed to look like. This is often the "sage on the stage" model, where the teacher is the one with all the knowledge and the students are receptacles for this knowledge. Although there's nothing inherently wrong with this approach, it becomes problematic when it's the only way you teach. Countless others have written about why educators shouldn't rely exclusively on this paradigm, such as Ted Dintersmith in *What School Could Be*,[11] so I won't go into detail about that here. Suffice it to say that, when executed effectively, hands-on learning that addresses real-world problems favors what some have called the "guide on the side" approach, although the educator still acts as the "sage on the stage" to teach the necessary skills. With careful planning and some built-in wiggle room to allow changes on the go, you'll absolutely be able to create a learning experience for your students that is rigorous — the "exhaustive" kind of rigor, rather than the "exhausting" kind.

- **It takes too much time.** I've heard this one a lot, mostly from teachers who haven't yet tried any of these frameworks. They worry that building a big project will take valuable time away from other content that they need to teach, with no guarantee that it will be worth it. Of course, big projects require a good chunk

---

11   Dintersmith, T. (2018) *What School Could Be: Insights and Inspiration from Teachers across America*, Princeton University Press

of time, but there's always the option of starting small. You could dip your toes in the water by designing a one-week PBL unit, for example, or perhaps even a three-day project. Regardless of how you begin, you'll need to familiarize yourself with the framework, connect with other educators about your idea(s), and set a firm end date for the project. After all, it's OK if your students don't finish everything you set out to accomplish. The point is the *process* of learning and working to create something. If you're committed to using a particular framework, creating a structured classroom environment, and involving other educators in the process then you can create a high-quality learning experience for your students that fits into almost any time period.

These criticisms are common ones and of course there are others. Most raise reasonable concerns. If you're a teacher who's thinking about employing hands-on learning that addresses real-world problems, you must consider them. And if you're an administrator working with teachers on advancing this approach to learning, it's important to ask those teachers if they've considered them. This way there's a much greater chance of success for all involved.

One last point on this topic. As with any good teaching unit, you also need to consider and include the basic elements of unit planning. Doing so ensures that you teach specific skills, maintain a structured classroom environment, keep the rigor, and do it all in your desired timeframe.

Here are the basics to keep in mind.

1. Decide how you want your students to show their learning at the end of the unit. What will the final product be? How will it function as a summative assessment?

2. Identify the understanding goals that will help you determine which specific skills to teach. If applicable, align with standards.

3. Design lessons and activities to be used throughout the unit in order to teach the skills you identified and therefore help your students reach their understanding goals.

4. Design formative assessments to evaluate your students' learning throughout the unit.

With a critical mind and careful planning, you can absolutely be successful with hands-on learning that addresses real-world problems.

A word about makerspaces

Each of the frameworks I've outlined in this chapter requires — or at the very least strongly encourages — students to create something that shows their learning. Because school librarians often lead the charge in terms of bringing about hands-on learning that addresses real-world problems, and because today's school libraries are increasingly flexible learning spaces, you'll often see makerspaces inside school libraries. This isn't always the case, of course, and each school's unique needs and constraints should ultimately determine where the makerspace lives. Regardless, they're perfect for all schools interested in facilitating hands-on learning that addresses real-world problems. School librarians were early adopters of makerspaces because they simply make sense for facilitating this kind of learning.

Makerspaces provide the means through which students can use their imaginations, and their hands, to create. And students *creating* is obviously a crucial element in each of the frameworks we've discussed. In *Transforming Libraries*, Ron Starker makes the case:

> There are very few areas within today's schools where project-based learning can take place. You need open space, proper tools, building materials, and safety procedures to support maker spaces, design centers, and tinkering corners. And while I'm not proposing that we convert all our libraries into wood shops, I am suggesting that libraries can support the establishment of learning spaces to facilitate knowledge creation.[12]

That said, whether or not the makerspace lives in the school library is ultimately irrelevant. The important part is that any educator interested in hands-on learning that addresses real-world problems has a makerspace that they can use with their students. Providing space for students to innovate is what matters. After all, as David Kelley notes in the foreword to *Make Space*, it doesn't matter "whether it's a classroom

---

12   Starker, R. (2017) *Transforming Libraries: A Toolkit for Innovators, Makers, and Seekers*, Grafo Education

or the offices of a billion-dollar company, space is something to think of as an instrument for innovation and collaboration."[13]

School libraries leading the way

Now I'll introduce you to some forward-thinking school librarians who are employing hands-on learning that addresses real-world problems. I'll share an example from my own teaching practice and some examples from other school librarians throughout the US. We are not the only educators implementing this pedagogical approach, of course. But many of us are leaders in this area because, as I mentioned in the beginning of this chapter, it's the kind of teaching that plays to our strengths and helps us most effectively deliver the skills that today's school librarians aim to teach.

At my school, I have co-developed what has been dubbed "the Passion Project" with our fifth-grade class. For one hour each week, throughout the entire school year, the technology integrationist and I co-facilitate this course in collaboration with the fifth-grade homeroom teachers. With our help, students:

- Choose a topic they want to learn more about.
- Develop an argument — a thesis — related to their chosen topic.
- Use the research process to identify as many facts as possible that support their thesis.
- Communicate these facts through four pieces of writing, in different genres, and one physical representation of those ideas (painting, 3D-printed model, etc.).
- Make sure each piece of writing adheres to the conventions of its genre. If it's a newspaper article, it should look like a newspaper article. If it's a short scene from a play, it should look like a play script.
- Accompany their physical representation with a short artist's statement in which they explain how their artistic choices attempt to communicate certain facts.

13   Doorley, S. & Witthoft, S. (2012) *Make Space: How to Set the Stage for Creative Collaboration*, Wiley

- Create a website using Google Sites to house and display all their work and cite their sources.
- Create an in-person or virtual museum — we've done both — at the end of the year in which they publicly share their work with our school community: parents, teachers, and other students.

The entire project was essentially inspired by Tom Romano's *Blending Genre, Altering Style: Writing Multigenre Papers*, which had motivated me years earlier, when I was still teaching English, to experiment with multigenre research papers with my middle school students. After I assumed the role of school librarian, the technology team and I sought to reinvent — and better integrate — the library and technology curriculum at our school. During those discussions, I realized that the premise of the multigenre research paper could be helpful as we began to think about research-based projects.

Here's Romano's definition of a multigenre research paper.

> *A multigenre paper arises from research, experience, and imagination. It is not an uninterrupted, expository monolog nor a seamless narrative nor a collection of poems. A multigenre paper is composed of many genres and subgenres, each piece self-contained, making a point of its own, yet connected by theme or topic and sometimes by language, images, and content. In addition to many genres, a multigenre research paper may also contain many voices, not just the author's. The trick is to make such a paper hang together.*[14]

Clearly, we have taken the idea of a multigenre research paper and scaled it up to a year-long research project, and various digital platforms have become the mediums through which students share their writing. It has been a lot of fun and a lot of work, especially for our students. The Passion Project has essentially evolved into a capstone experience for our lower school students because they finish right before stepping up to middle school.

Each student is assigned a project advisor dedicated to helping them throughout the year. The three fifth-grade teachers serve as advisors,

---

14   Romano, T. (2000) *Blending Genre, Altering Style: Writing Multigenre Papers*, Boynton/Cook Publishers

as do the technology integrationist and I. The project advisor's role is to guide students and use our jointly created checklist to ensure that each student makes adequate progress on every step of the year-long process. The fifth-grade teachers' involvement is limited to the advisory role. The technology integrationist and I are in charge of designing and facilitating the course.

We begin each class with a mini-lesson, with the technology integrationist taking the lead on lessons related to technology and me taking the lead on lessons related to research and writing. As the school librarian, it's wonderful to have the opportunity to work with students throughout the entire research process. I show them how to find good information using Google, age-appropriate academic databases, books, and e-books. I also show students how to reach out to experts on their topic, by networking within our school community or drafting a cordial email to someone whose work they found online. And, of course, I teach the part that always makes them jump for joy: how to keep track of and properly cite their sources.

Part of what gives this project its energy is its sheer ambition. We're asking students to do a lot — there are many moving parts and there's plenty to keep in mind as they work. But they're studying something they're truly excited to study, and they're working to express themselves imaginatively and create a final product that will be shared with a real audience. For these reasons, students are fully engaged. Sure, they tire of certain stages at certain points (not citing sources, of course), but their feedback at the end of the year is overwhelmingly positive.

It's this energy that makes hands-on learning that addresses real-world problems so powerful, for teachers and students alike. Momentum builds quickly and there's almost always enough to last through long-term projects. For me, one of the best parts is the ongoing opportunity to collaborate with my colleagues. We're constantly learning from each other and inspiring each other with new ideas, and this kind of back and forth between educators can be the spark necessary to make this kind of learning possible for students.

Forward-thinking librarians

Meg B. Allison, school librarian at U-32 Middle & High School in Montpelier, Vermont, works hard to build relationships with the other educators in her school, and those relationships often result in collaborative teaching projects. By prioritizing hands-on learning that addresses real-world problems, Allison helps students learn the 21st century library skills they need in order to be informed, productive, and resourceful citizens who have the ability — and the drive — to make a positive impact on the world.

Each year, Allison has her middle school students research a local mountain and produce a digital guidebook for that mountain. Students hike and record data on soil samples, tree height, and more. They analyze and graph this data in science class. In English class, students read *Lost on a Mountain in Maine* by Donn Fendler and write poems to be included in the guidebooks. Allison teaches students how to effectively use content-creation tools like Canva and Google Slides to design the guidebooks. When students finish, they present their work to the Vermont Agency of Natural Resources, and the agency publishes their guidebooks online.

Allison has also spearheaded numerous other learning projects at her school. When students returned to in-person classes during the Covid-19 pandemic, the school library itself was still closed, so Allison worked with a high school humanities teacher to have students design a "Library Books To Go" program. Allison gave her students this real problem to address and they designed a plan to make books available to the school community. An in-house marketing plan was also executed by students, which involved making buttons for faculty and students to wear, designing Instagram posts for the school's feed, and creating eye-catching informational posters for display throughout the school.

It's this kind of innovation that makes hands-on learning that addresses real-world problems so clearly worthwhile. Allison describes this kind of learning as "sticky" — it stays with students for many years. She argues that students may not remember what they wrote in an essay, but they'll likely remember what they learned through a hands-on project. Allison also notes that addressing real-world problems leads to increased student engagement, and with that comes creative problem-solving.

Erika Long, school librarian at Thurgood Marshall Middle School in Nashville, Tennessee, is leading the charge to bring hands-on learning that addresses real-world problems to her students. At her previous school, she was part of a committee that researched project-based learning. She led the effort to spread awareness of how PBL works and ensure that teachers and students alike had access to the resources they needed to make this approach to learning possible. Her biggest priority was helping students formulate questions:

- What's the (real-world) problem?
- What created — or led to — the problem?
- What have others already done to address it?
- How can they (students) help address it?

At Long's current school, she has spearheaded an effort to introduce and implement inquiry-based learning. This involves her working directly with teachers and students across subject areas and grade levels. Long tells me the implementation process isn't always easy. "It's all about tweaking as you go," she says. "And I've learned to involve teachers on the front end of the process, rather than trying to get them on board with something that's already rolling." This is certainly important to keep in mind for all educators interested in bringing any of these frameworks to their schools.

Long notes that student choice is at the center of this pedagogical approach to teaching and learning, from the questions that drive their projects to how they'll share their final products (or what Long's school calls "deliverables"). She argues that student choice motivates young people to dig into topics they're passionate about; in many cases it helps students who don't believe they're passionate about anything to successfully identify something they are excited to explore in more detail. For these students, she has found it helpful to pose this question: "If some friends were sitting around talking, what would they have to be talking about for you to be physically unable to not say something?" This is where these students have their "aha" moment, discovering they actually do have strong — even *passionate* — feelings about a variety of topics, such as concussions in sports and the gender pay gap. This self-discovery alone is invaluable.

Hands-on learning that addresses real-world problems also works very well at the elementary school level. Maura Madigan, school librarian at North Springfield Elementary School in Springfield, Virginia, writes in *School Library Journal* that she employs this approach in Kindergarten through fifth grade. She calls it project-based or problem-based learning, and to her the benefits are clear:

> *All my PBL projects have a hands-on component in which students physically create something. This increases engagement and allows students to show different strengths. Each initiative targets multiple curriculum standards and skills, such as collaboration, communication, critical and creative thinking, and resiliency. Learning how to work in a group, compromise, innovate, and overcome setbacks are all essential life skills that kids practice during PBL projects.*[15]

Madigan worked with her principal to move book checkout time outside of her 30-minute weekly library class period, so that students could use their limited class time for PBL. I've actually done the same for the elementary students at my Pre-K–8 school, so I can attest to the difference this change makes. Madigan coordinates projects based on what's happening in each grade's classroom, or by doing in-depth research on a particular topic in library class and then embarking on a project related to that topic. For example, her Kindergarteners do a deep dive into fairy tales and then "build 'just right' chairs for Goldilocks."

Like the other two school librarians I've spotlighted in this section, Madigan notes that collaborating with colleagues is key. With her Kindergarten project, for example, it's as elemental as requiring help from other educators so that one adult isn't in sole charge of a room full of Kindergarteners using glue guns and staplers. Collaboration begins there and blossoms into incredible learning opportunities. It's what makes this approach work so well.

---

15   Madigan, M. (2018) "Eight project-based learning activities for your school library," *School Library Journal*. www.slj.com/eight-project-based-learning-activities-for-your-school-library

Takeaways for all educators

We've seen how forward-thinking school librarians are educational leaders in prioritizing hands-on learning that addresses real-world problems. Because this approach to learning is so valuable to all students, it's necessary for us to consider how educators of all stripes — teachers and administrators — can utilize this approach.

For teachers, no matter where you fall on the spectrum of experience, you can begin by considering which parts of your curriculum could most benefit from being revamped. Or you might consider which part of your curriculum you're most passionate about. After all, on the front end of any kind of learning experience, the teachers' level of interest and enthusiasm makes all the difference. And it's arguably even more important with the approach we're discussing here, because it's often a relatively new experience for students and teachers alike. The more positive energy you bring to planning and introducing it, the better the experience will be for everyone.

Once you've decided where in your curriculum you could employ hands-on learning that addresses real-world problems, you should determine which standards or understanding goals you will use. Then consider who could help your students achieve these goals. Maybe there are a few opportunities for interdisciplinary collaboration. Or, depending on the nature of your project, you might consider collaborating with a technology teacher, librarian, and/or art teacher. If any of these other educators are excited about your project, they might even be willing to co-teach with you on a daily or weekly basis. You could also find and tap other educators online who might offer additional guidance, or even authors and experts who might be willing to visit your classroom virtually to help inspire or guide your students.

Remember, collaboration is the lifeblood of hands-on learning that addresses real-world problems. It's how this kind of learning comes — and stays — alive. You benefit from having another educator's perspective on the project, your students benefit from having another voice in the room to guide them in the learning process. It's the epitome of a win-win.

For administrators, you might begin by considering *where* and *how* you're creating space for hands-on learning that addresses real-world problems. If it's not happening yet, or if it is but it's rare, you might offer valuable in-house professional development opportunities for your teaching staff. For example, my school leadership team has consistently provided teachers with opportunities to learn more about design thinking, through interactive presentations and workshops at our school and beyond. Not everyone will buy in, but once teachers are given permission to experiment with this approach then many will jump at the opportunity, no matter which framework you and/or your school decide to focus on. Inevitably, if they're well-supported, educators will find that they and their students have a very positive experience with this approach. These educators, in turn, become your evangelists. Also, if your school doesn't have a makerspace, empower interested educators in your school to start one. Reallocate space, if necessary, but make sure one exists somewhere.

For both teachers and administrators, I recommend choosing one of the frameworks discussed in this chapter to address any actual problems you're currently dealing with in your role. For example, if you're a social studies teacher who's tired of a unit on World War II, you might consider using design thinking with the colleagues in your department to create a brand new product (teaching unit) for your users (students). And perhaps the design thinking process you use will result in designing a WWII design thinking project for your students. How meta!

Or perhaps you're an administrator who would like to launch a particular initiative. You might consider enlisting interested teachers to work together, or directly with you, using the inquiry-based learning framework as your guide. In partnership, you'll ask questions and investigate possible answers. Then you'll create something that can be shared with your entire school community. After reflecting on your process together, you might consider sharing your reflections during a faculty meeting, thereby modeling the power and efficacy of inquiry-based learning for all your faculty and staff. Honestly, other than giving a group of educators opportunities to experiment with this approach themselves, I can't think of a better way to "sell" hands-on learning that addresses real-world problems.

As Mike Rose reminds us in *Why School?*, "[a] good education helps us make sense of the world and find our way in it."[16] Hands-on learning that addresses real-world problems provides a good education for our students precisely because it brings the world outside school *into* school — and because we trust ourselves and our students enough to know they will indeed find their way through this authentic, messy, and exciting process.

How your school librarian can help

If you're a teacher who's interested in getting started, school librarians want to help. And if you've already started, we still want to help. In *Leading from the Library*, Shannon McClintock Miller and William Bass stress our capacity for collaborating with our fellow educators:

> *Collaboration is one of the skills required for literacy in today's world, and librarians are master collaborators. We see it in the co-planning of lessons and sharing of resources that impact what and how students learn. Collaboration is a skill that is honed over time, but it's also a skill that is central to library programs throughout the world.*[17]

Below are specific ways you can tap your school librarian to help you with hands-on learning that addresses real-world problems.

- **Brainstorming.** Teachers and administrators, you can come to us with any ideas you have related to this approach to teaching and learning. We can be helpful with the ideation process for several reasons. We work across grade levels and subject areas, so we have a bird's-eye view of what's happening throughout the school. Accordingly, we can help you identify available opportunities and resources of which you might not be aware. We also have direct access to resources — technology, information databases, etc. — that can help you get started. And finally, we enjoy the nerdy back and forth and can provide the support you need to get your learning project off the ground.

16   Rose, M. (2009) *Why School? Reclaiming Education for All of Us*, The New Press
17   McClintock Miller, S. & Bass, W. (2019) *Leading from the Library: Help Your School Community Thrive in the Digital Age*, International Society for Technology in Education

- **Content curation.** We're experts at finding good information and good resources, both of which are essential for success with hands-on learning that addresses real-world problems. We can pull together relevant websites, books and e-books, teaching materials, and more that will save you time and provide you and your students with further inspiration and motivation. Our curating work can also help you scaffold specific parts of the learning process for students who could use the additional support.

- **Co-teaching.** Our availability often differs greatly from school to school, and from day to day. But many of us are available and eager to co-teach with you, often throughout the entirety of a project — even if it's only coming in once a week to teach specific research or digital literacy skills that are relevant to the learning and creating. I can honestly say that as a school librarian, my most exciting teaching units have involved co-teaching with classroom teachers over the course of a longer-term project. It's an ideal situation: the educators and the students are all learning from each other and working toward common goals. There's nothing better than that.

- **Advising.** Perhaps you've already started a project, or maybe you're at a stage where it would be useful to have students receive feedback from another educator on their ideas, processes, or creations. Let us know what kind of feedback you're looking for and we'll be happy to deliver it. In this way, our desks often transform into something like the Genius Bar at the Apple Store. Not to say we're geniuses, but we really are helpful in this kind of advising and/or problem-solving role. Also, when we perform this kind of role, we can provide the resources that we're skilled at curating and sharing.

- **Library space.** Many school libraries can be used as collaborative learning spaces. In fact, many have been designed, or redesigned, for exactly this purpose. We're happy to have you use the library space for whatever you have in mind. In most school libraries, you can formally or informally "book" the space (I swear the pun was unintentional) for set periods of time. Also, as mentioned earlier in the chapter, in many schools the library actually contains a makerspace, offering helpful tools and materials for the "making" part of the learning process. At my school we have a makerspace that's separate from the library, but teachers will use the library as a learning space just because it's full of resources, like books, technology, and, well, librarians. Just having all this help at the ready is as good a reason as any to take advantage of your school library as a space for hands-on learning that addresses real-world problems.

If you're an administrator who's interested in bringing hands-on learning that addresses real-world problems to your school, or expanding the work that's already being done in this area, consider giving the educators in your school the time and space they need to collaborate across subject areas and divisions, with the ultimate goal of creating interdisciplinary units of study that utilize this approach. From the very beginning, your school librarian is the perfect professional to consult. We can provide you with the research that backs up the effectiveness of this approach. Because of our bird's-eye view of classes and curriculum, we can help you identify how and where pilot projects might be most successful. And we can help you teach the faculty about it, including specific digital and/or technological skills that might make your efforts more successful.

The bottom line is that we're here and we're ready to help our fellow educators transform schools. Across the world, our students are waiting.

Becoming curious

To end this chapter, I'll return to the beginning: Rob Bell's epigraph describes curiosity as underrated. Indeed, by prioritizing hands-on learning that addresses real-world problems, educators tap into the innate curiosity of everyone involved. This is how innovation begins.

When we prioritize this pedagogical approach, students learn to follow and trust their curiosity as they develop their own questions and create their own answers. The educators designing and supporting these learning experiences find that they too become more curious — about their students, curriculum, teaching goals, and even their own passions outside school.

Teachers and administrators, below are a few questions to guide your thinking more specifically toward prioritizing hands-on learning that addresses real-world problems.

Teachers:

- Which aspects of hands-on learning that addresses real-world problems appeal to you the most and why?
- How does this pedagogical approach align with your own professional goals?
- Which part of your curriculum could most benefit from being revamped?
- Who could you collaborate with to bring this approach to life in your class(es)?
- How can you make sure there's a real, live audience to observe or experience whatever your students create?
- What resources do you need today in order to take the first step?

Administrators:

- How could hands-on learning that addresses real-world problems help you bring about innovation in your school?
- Does your school have a makerspace or some kind of collaborative workspace that teachers and students could use to accommodate this pedagogical approach?
- How can you provide your faculty with the time they need to collaborate with each other and plan to implement this approach?
- If most of the faculty has little or no experience with this pedagogical approach, how could you ensure buy-in?
- What kinds of professional development opportunities can you provide that might help?
- How could you use one of the frameworks (project-based learning, design thinking, or inquiry-based learning) in your own leadership practice? How could you share your experience with it as a model for your faculty?

Chapter 2

Improving access to books, information, and technology

"Access to knowledge is the superb, the supreme act of truly great civilizations"

— Toni Morrison

As a resident of the Greater Boston area, I live quite close to the first two free libraries in the world: the Peterborough Town Library in Peterborough, New Hampshire, and the Boston Public Library. There's clearly a rich tradition here of improving public access to information. Thanks to these early pioneers, intellectual freedom has become a basic human right here and in many other places throughout the world.

Within their schools, school libraries perform a similar function to public libraries. The American Library Association puts it like this:

The school library plays a unique role in promoting, protecting, and educating about intellectual freedom. It serves as a point of voluntary access to information and ideas and as a learning laboratory for students as they acquire critical thinking and problem-solving skills needed in a pluralistic society. Although the educational level and program of the school necessarily shape the resources and services of a school library, the principles of the American Library Association's Library Bill of Rights apply equally to all libraries, including school libraries. Under these principles, all students have equitable access to library facilities, resources, and instructional programs.[18]

School librarians work hard to improve access to books and information. And information, of course, is increasingly available through various forms of technology. As such, school librarians are also charged with improving access to technology. This is incredibly important work — essential, even — that we do on behalf of students and faculty, and we've become increasingly innovative in how we do it.

This chapter explores how school libraries are improving access to books, information, and technology for their schools and why all educators should keep access to these resources top of mind in their respective roles. I'll begin by defining exactly what I mean by book access, information access, and technology access, followed by a brief explanation of how all this relates to the movement toward democratizing education.

I'll walk you through some of the work I've done to improve access at my school, as well as highlight the inspiring work of other school librarians across the US. Then I'll share ideas about how all educators can improve access, no matter your teaching or administrative role, and some recommendations for how to leverage your school librarian to guide and assist in these efforts.

Book access

All schools want their students to have access to books, yet many school libraries are understaffed and underfunded. On top of this, many classrooms have a severe shortage of books. Providing book access means ensuring that all students in any given school have as many opportunities as possible to read age-appropriate books. This starts with the bookshelves in the school library, where librarians have expertly curated collections that are rich, diverse, and of interest to their student population.

---

18   American Library Association. *Access to Resources and Services in the School Library: An Interpretation of the Library Bill of Rights*, adopted July 2, 1986, by the ALA Council. www.ala.org/advocacy/intfreedom/librarybill/interpretations/accessresources

Book access must also involve classroom libraries. There has been some debate about whether or not classroom libraries diminish the role of school libraries. But school libraries and classroom libraries are not — and cannot be — mutually exclusive. As educators, we can all agree that what's most important is for students to have access to an abundance of books. Therefore, books must live in classrooms in addition to school libraries, especially considering that classrooms are where students spend most of their time while in school. School librarians can and should help teachers with classroom libraries, which I'll discuss later in this chapter.

E-books are important in any conversation about book access. Although they require an internet connection and a device of some kind, either or both of which can be prohibitive for some students, e-books are generally a fantastic way to grant students access to books. Many school libraries offer a selection of e-books, either through some kind of free, state-sponsored consortium, like we have here in Massachusetts, or through a purchased collection via a company like OverDrive, referrals to public library websites, or a combination of these. No matter how access is provided, what's important is that access exists and students understand how to browse, download, and open the e-books.

Book access cannot be provided without adequate funding. It's the responsibility of school boards, administrators, superintendents, and national educational leaders to ensure that schools have enough resources to staff their libraries with librarians and fill their classroom libraries with books. It's beyond ridiculous that many schools have had their school librarian and/or librarian aide positions cut. It's also beyond ridiculous that many schools do not provide librarians with a book budget or classroom teachers with stipends for classroom libraries. If it's our goal as educators to help young people evolve into well-read, knowledgeable young people who can become tomorrow's leaders, then we need to properly invest in them. We need to shout this from the rooftops!

In *Game Changer!*, Donalyn Miller and Colby Sharp write: "Without access to books, the persistent gap between children who have access and those who don't will remain. Our students will not reach their full potential without books, regardless of the educational reforms schools implement."[19] For many students, their futures depend on their access to books. After all, like education in general, literacy is nothing if not a form of liberation.

Information access

In the context of schools, information access is the ability of students to find information and successfully make use of it. Information access is a form of intellectual freedom and it's important across subject areas. Although all K-12 schools work to provide information access to students, many schools also limit and in some cases restrict the information made available to them.

Librarians have long been ambassadors of information access and I would argue that all educators should care deeply about it. After all, access means opportunity. Whatever your role in the world of education, providing your students with more opportunities to become knowledgeable and self-sufficient is paramount in our collective effort to help them find their voice and use it effectively.

The American Association of School Librarians (AASL) clearly defines the right that students have to access information: "Learners have the freedom to speak and hear what others have to say, rather than allowing others to control their access to ideas and information; the school librarian's responsibility is to develop these dispositions in learners, educators, and all other members of the learning community."[20]

The school librarian is crucial in the effort to provide information access to students. It's at the core of what we do. School librarians help students understand that they have a right to information that enlightens them about topics of personal interest, as well as information that helps them achieve success in their academic coursework. Books are one way students access information, of course. But the internet is the primary way.

Librarians create access to information through various modalities, including online databases, magazines, and librarian-curated online

19   Miller, D. & Sharp, C. (2018) *Game Changer! Book Access for All Kids*, Scholastic
20   American Association of School Librarians. (2018) *AASL Standards Framework for Learners*, American Library Association. https://standards.aasl.org/wp-content/uploads/2017/11/AASL-Standards-Framework-for-Learners-pamphlet.pdf

resource collections. In terms of access, this is a wonderful thing. In *The School Library Manager*, the authors explain what information access has meant historically and what it means right now:

> *One of the traditional responsibilities of information professionals in all types of libraries is identifying, evaluating, acquiring, and organizing information resources to meet the needs of their patrons. At one time, these resources were primarily in print and non-print formats; however, the expansion of resources made possible by advances in technology now makes information available to users in libraries, schools, offices, and homes and requires new approaches to managing information. Library users now expect to have information available to them beyond the walls of the physical space and accessible 24/7.*[21]

There's a very real need for professional guidance when it comes to having students navigate the huge, amazing, terrifying mess that is the internet. Almost all students use Google, but not many know how to use it well. Fake news and conspiracy theories are proliferating rapidly, and it's more and more difficult to discern facts from opinions. Social media algorithms continue to show "content" — the buzzword for information — based on what the algorithms determine to be relevant to the user. These are significant issues, and schools must equip students with the skills they need to understand and navigate them.

For this reason, we cannot separate information access from the professionals who work to provide it in our schools. Let's not mince words: equipping students with the ability to understand and use information effectively is an integral element of information access. It's how we enable them to become free thinkers and therefore free citizens.

Technology access

Technology access refers to providing students with the means through which they can access and create information. Access to technology is a necessary part of leveling the playing field for all students. This means doing everything possible to make sure students have access at school

---

21   Woolls, B., Carlson Weeks, A. & Coatney, S. (2014) *The School Library Manager* (fifth edition), Libraries Unlimited

and at home to technology that enables them to complete their assigned coursework effectively and efficiently.

As someone who works at an independent school with more than adequate technological resources, I'm acutely aware of how money buys access to technology and how financial disparities widen the education gap. It's grossly unfair. According to a 2018 study by the Pew Research Center, "one-third of households with children ages 6 to 17 and whose annual income falls below $30,000 a year do not have a high-speed internet connection at home, compared with just 6% of such households earning $75,000 or more a year."[22] The resulting educational gap is often referred to as the digital divide, with many students unable to complete homework as a result. This problem became increasingly visible as schools shifted to online learning during the Covid-19 pandemic.

Right now, technology access is an ideal that is successfully achieved by some and seemingly impossible for many. But given the tech-centric nature of many new jobs, schools must do everything they can to make technology access a mandate. There are some concrete steps that can be taken to ensure that students at least have opportunities to use technology while in school, including but not limited to:

- Applying for grants that provide tablets and laptops, or the money to purchase them.
- Making computer labs or libraries available during study halls or other breaks in students' schedules.
- Creating after-school programs and electives centered around technological and digital literacy.
- Facilitating hands-on learning (project-based learning, design thinking, or inquiry-based learning) that addresses the real-world problem of lack of technology access.
- Doing everything possible to ensure the funding of school technology departments and libraries.

---

22   Anderson, M. & Perrin, A. (2018) "Nearly one-in-five teens can't always finish their homework because of the digital divide," Pew Research Center, www.pewresearch. org/fact-tank/2018/10/26/nearly-one-in-five-teens-cant-always-finish-their-homework-because-of-the-digital-divide

The first four steps are important, but they are essentially stopgaps. The last step is probably the only way long-term, positive change will occur. This is true not only for technology access but also book and information access.

Democratizing education

Whenever we talk about leveling the playing field for all students, or making sure all students have access to books, information, and technology, we are talking about democratizing education. This concept really is as simple and radical as it sounds. It means applying the principles of democracy — particularly the democratic principle of social equality — to the world of education. It seems logical that if we want our students to help keep democracy alive after they graduate, then we ought to perpetuate it ourselves in the way we educate them.

By and large, this involves making sure they know they have a voice in the learning process and that they can use that voice to change the world for the better.

We must also keep in mind that access should always extend to students with impairments and disabilities. According to the DO-IT (Disabilities, Opportunities, Internetworking, and Technology) Center at the University of Washington:

> *Some methods used to impart information are not accessible to some students, including those with visual impairments, hearing impairments, mobility impairments, speech impairments, learning disabilities, and health impairments. Those whose first language is not English or who have alternative learning styles also face difficulties in accessing some types of information.*[23]

It is essential, then, that schools take into account the diverse needs of their students when it comes to improving access to books, information, and technology. This work must be an ongoing collaboration between classroom teachers, special education teachers, technology specialists, librarians, and administrators.

When we make sure all students have access to the resources they need, we give them possibilities. We create innumerable paths for them to

---

23   www.washington.edu/doit/information-access-0

discover how others make sense of the world, so they can come to make sense of it themselves. By providing access to books, we give them the possibilities that accompany exploring new worlds, new ideas, and, best of all, new questions. By providing access to information and technology, we give them the possibilities that accompany connecting with — and participating in — the global learning community.

Improving access is important to the effort to democratize education, and school libraries are advancing this work in impressive ways. But before I share how, let's address head-on some of the roadblocks you might face in your own efforts to improve access to books, information, and technology at your school.

Roadblocks

Improving access in schools can be difficult, but it doesn't have to be. Below, I list some of the problems that you'll likely face in your efforts to improve access in your department, school, or district. For each, I also include some advice on how to deal with the roadblock.

Lack of funding for school libraries and/or classroom libraries

Many school librarians have tiny budgets for huge student populations. Some school librarians are not given *any money at all* for books, which, of course, is even more absurd. This problem should be a call to action for all educators, because it affects all educators. If we want our students to have access to books, the very first step is giving school librarians the money they need to fill bookshelves. Unfunded libraries are forced to turn to book fairs, parent donations, and grants. And although these efforts to improve book access are laudable, the problem itself is unacceptable.

For classroom libraries, many teachers have turned to crowdfunding to purchase books. On Twitter, teachers share their wishlists with the hashtag #ClearTheLists in the hope of receiving support from friends and strangers. We can do better. We *must* do better. To help fund school libraries, visit Save School Librarians (www.saveschoollibrarians.org), which links to petitions and forms you can fill out to email your state representatives. These options are quick and easy, and they really can make a difference.

To help fund classroom libraries, the high school teacher and Project LIT founder Jarred Amato recommends that you sign up and request support at www.fbmarketplace.org/register. In an interview with *Edutopia*, Amato also suggests you schedule a meeting with your principal or school leadership team and "share your vision for bringing more classroom library books to your school. Schools often work to find money in their budget to purchase books. Asking is step one … you may be pleasantly surprised."[24]

Lack of funding for technology

Some schools, like mine, have 1:1 device programs where students have direct and constant access to a computer, either in the form of a laptop or tablet. This is the ideal, because students need computers to access much of the information that schools expect them to find. Yet 1:1 programs, crucial as they are, are still far from the norm. If you're looking for ways to increase technology access by securing funding for more or better technology, the educational technology specialist and consultant Dr. Sheryl Abshire provides assurance that you will be able to find a grant to fund your needs. In an interview with the International Society for Technology in Education (ISTE), she recommends four excellent resources for funding in the US. Below is the list of these resources, along with descriptions written by ISTE blogger Chris Frisella.

1. **Bank of America Foundation** (www.bankofamerica.com/foundation). "This foundation funds education with an emphasis on K-12, including after-school programs, early childhood development, English as a second language, financial literacy and youth mentoring programs."

2. **Computers for Learning** (www.computersforlearning.gov). "This program donates surplus federal computer equipment to schools and educational nonprofits, giving special consideration to those with the greatest need."

3. **George Lucas Educational Foundation** (www.edutopia.org). "Although not a source for funding, this site contains a myriad of sites and sources of information about grants."

---

24   Alber, R. (2019) "How to stock your classroom library," *Edutopia*, www.edutopia.org/article/how-stock-your-classroom-library

4. **Grants Information Collection** (https://grants.library.wisc.edu). "The University of Wisconsin maintains a comprehensive site with grant resources."[25]

Lack of staffing

To improve access to books, information, and technology, there must be librarian and technology specialist positions in every school. These education professionals are trained to spearhead and sustain access efforts, and if granted the ability to do so, they can be school leaders on this front. They can do much of the work in finding resources and funding. In order to do this work effectively, however, librarians and technology specialists must not be shared by multiple schools. They must not be part-time. And they must not be lumped into the same position. (In some schools, the librarian and technology specialist are essentially one and the same.)

While there is certainly some overlap in what librarians and technology specialists do, both have well-defined job responsibilities that largely serve different purposes. These need to be distinct, fully funded, full-time positions in order to provide the kind of support that students and teachers really need to improve access.

If your school doesn't have a school librarian, I recommend connecting with a group of like-minded colleagues and making your appeal directly to your administrator and/or superintendent. Save School Librarians, mentioned earlier, actively lobbies for school libraries and librarians, and even helps interested parties put forth "bills in their legislatures to mandate school librarians in each school."[26] I highly recommend visiting this site and getting involved.

Although an equivalent organization does not exist for technology specialists (school librarian positions are historically much more at risk than technology specialists), you can still do the work of connecting with like-minded colleagues and making your case to an administrator and/or superintendent. Likewise, you can contact your legislators through

---

25 Frisella, C. (2021) "Need an edtech grant? Then get writing!", ISTE, www.iste.org/explore/tools-devices-and-apps/need-edtech-grant-then-get-writing
26 www.saveschoollibrarians.org/about

a website such as https://openstates.org and make your case directly to them. It's unfair that in many places educators must also become activists in order to provide the kind of education that students need.

Fixed mindset

Sometimes we encounter in ourselves and in others an acceptance of the way things are, even when things aren't great. This isn't to say we don't care, because almost all educators care — it's why we do what we do. But I think it's worth contemplating the extent to which we sometimes unexpectedly and/or unintentionally settle for too little. I've certainly settled on countless occasions. Pushing back or pushing new agendas can be exhausting.

The thing is, when it comes to improving access to books, information, and technology for our students, there is always work to be done. And this work is always important. Granting students greater access connects them with resources that can help them learn and grow. The truth is that sometimes we just have to shift our mindset, so we can identify problems as problems and then find the motivation to address them. Access can always be improved.

Lack of collaboration

This is related to the fixed mindset problem, in that there is an opportunity to improve access that hasn't yet been realized. Some schools technically have the professional and financial resources to improve access, but because of a lack of collaboration between educators, access isn't what it could and should be. It is all too easy for us to stay in our silos, and I've been just as guilty of this as anyone. But when we feel strongly about something — in this case, access — it's critical that we connect with colleagues who might be interested and/or able to help. For example, if you're an administrator at a school in which some classrooms have libraries and others don't, you might consider convening your school librarian and teachers to create an initiative in which every student has access to books in every classroom. Or, if you're a classroom teacher who knows that funds might be available in your school or district for your students to have devices, connect with your principal and technology specialist (if there is one) and draw up a proposal. Write emails. Coordinate meetings. Start committees.

What I'm speaking of here is basically activism within the school and it can absolutely yield results. Examples abound of teachers and administrators who feel passionately about a particular problem and work together to address it. I highly recommend rallying any and all colleagues around the cause of improving access for students. Because even in schools where access doesn't seem to be an issue, there are many ways to increase it for the benefit of students. I'll explain more about how to do this in the next section.

These roadblocks are only some of those you may encounter in your efforts to improve access to books, information, and technology. There are others, of course. The bottom line is that access can always be improved and there are always ways to do it.

School libraries leading the way

School librarians work tirelessly to improve access to books, information, and technology. In numerous studies over the years, these efforts have been shown to lead to positive outcomes for students. In an article in *Phi Delta Kappan* about the research-backed benefits attributed to school library programs, Keith Curry Lance and Debra E. Kachel explain that "[students] tend to thrive academically where library programs provide ready access to free and subscription-based online resources alongside more traditional collections of books, periodicals, and audiovisual resources."[27] These efforts really do make a difference.

First, let me share some of the ways that, as a school librarian, I've helped increase access at my school. Bear in mind that my school has plenty of resources, but, as we know, access can always be improved and we should always work to do so. When I assumed my role as librarian, one of the first things I did was work to revitalize the school library website. This was a top priority because a school library's website, if designed properly, can grant students (and teachers and parents, for that matter) access to all sorts of information resources from anywhere inside or outside the school.

---

27   Curry Lance, K. & Kachel, D.E. (2018) "Why school librarians matter: what years of research tell us," *Phi Delta Kappan*, https://kappanonline.org/lance-kachel-school-librarians-matter-years-research

I connected with a colleague who manages the school website, and she kindly helped me make a visually clean library website interface that's easy to navigate, even for our early elementary students. The site links to our e-book collection, to a form for our birthday book program (in which parents or guardians donate a book in their child's name for the child's birthday), to our student-staffed and library-sanctioned writing center, and to subscription databases. When students were unable to visit the library during the Covid-19 pandemic, we added a link to a form that students, parents, and teachers could fill out to request books. This addition was necessary to keep library books in circulation, but it has been so well received that we plan to keep it.

I also enlisted the help of a few colleagues in our technology department to work with Follett, the company that hosts our library catalog and book borrowing/checkout system, to obtain the source code necessary to install a simple search bar at the top of the library website homepage. This allows all our constituents — students, faculty, and parents alike — to access our entire book catalog from anywhere. Everyone can see what books we have and how many copies of each are available at any given time. This increased access to our book collection, coupled with easy, quick access to e-books and databases in which students can access information and entertainment, has effectively expanded our resources well beyond the walls of our physical library. At all times, students have access to important information they can use to help complete their coursework and/or dig into content of personal interest.

Another way I've worked to increase access to books and information is by creating new opportunities for students and faculty to be physically in the library. My thinking is that if I can get them in here, they will see the resources we have available and become much more likely to use them.

For example, one of the first things I did as librarian was coordinate with our elementary and middle school division heads to open up the library to students for recess and study halls. We can't have all students in the library all the time — the space is far from huge — so we can only extend this option to certain grade levels on certain days. A faculty member is present to supervise the students who choose to use the library during this time — an alternative to supervising students in the playground.

Perhaps unsurprisingly, the faculty members who are assigned to the library for recess duty love it. It's a chance for them, too, to poke around, read a bit, and chat casually with students.

I should probably mention that our school library, like many other 21st century school libraries, is very much *not* a "shushy" place. To illustrate this point, in the event that a student or faculty member walks in when the library is otherwise quiet, I often have music with a beat playing. It's not loud and it's almost always instrumental, but it does show that this isn't the kind of library that worships silence. On the contrary: the 21st century school library is often a collaborative workspace. In our middle school, we have two study hall options for students: silent and collaborative (where, as necessary, they're allowed to work together on group projects). I successfully lobbied our middle school division head to move the collaborative study hall for each grade to the library. A middle school faculty member has always been assigned to these collaborative study halls — now they're assigned to supervise their students in the library.

During middle school study hall periods, I run and supervise a student-staffed writing center. I've trained a group of eighth-grade students to help other students, in grades five through eight, with their writing. Students who want help simply "sign out" of their normal study hall room and head to the library to work with student mentor writers throughout the brainstorming, drafting, and revision/editing processes. In effect, the eighth-grade students who staff the writing center are human resources. They know the information — how to write well — and the library provides other students with direct access to these human resources. At many times throughout the day, the library is a bustling, collaborative workspace where students come to learn with and from each other.

Another way our library space has been used to increase access is by hosting division and department meetings. For example, our library has hosted numerous professional development events as well as the bi-weekly middle school division meetings, resulting in numerous teachers seeing and taking advantage of various library resources — including the librarian! In terms of the physical library space, increased access absolutely equals increased awareness and usage of the books, information, and technology resources that we provide. Therefore, I can't stress enough the importance of using the school library as a meeting place for faculty on a regular basis. It's one of the crucial ways that the library becomes the hub of the school. After all, if faculty and administrators understand it as such, they will help students understand it this way, too. There's no question that advocating for the school library to be used as a collaborative workspace for students and faculty can lead to increased access.

Setting up self-checkout computers has been a huge help in increasing access to books, too. This was yet another collaboration between myself and my extremely helpful colleagues in our school's technology department, and it's ultimately pretty simple to set up. We repurposed two older computer monitors, purchased Google Chromebits (which are, in effect, inexpensive USB-stick-sized computers) and USB hub-splitters, and then hooked up the Chromebits, keyboards, mice, and barcode scanners. The two self-checkout computers sit side by side on a table adjacent to our circulation desk. It's incredibly helpful to have these machines available for students and/or faculty who swing by to borrow books when I'm out and about — teaching in a classroom, meeting with other teachers, etc.

I would also argue that this gives students and faculty a sense of ownership — self-reliance, even — when it comes to accessing the library. At the beginning of each school year, I teach new faculty and students in grades two through eight how to use the self-checkout machines, and although many of them need reminders throughout the year, this option has proven to be helpful and popular.

In terms of increasing access to technology in particular, I've organized a device-borrowing program for our school. Behind our circulation desk, I keep a supply of "loaner" laptops, laptop chargers, and phone chargers. Despite being a 1:1 school, we still have plenty of students and teachers who forget a device or charger, or whose device isn't working properly so they need to borrow a different one. Our technology department provides these devices and chargers, and helps troubleshoot any problems that arise with them. We are also privileged enough to have a portable cart of iPads that students can check out and use at school or, with a parent's permission, at home. Faculty members can borrow the entire cart whenever they need a group or class to use iPads for a particular lesson or project. These devices ensure that students and faculty have access to the technology they need to access the information they need.

Forward-thinking librarians

Julia Torres is a teacher librarian in Denver for the Montbello Campus, which serves five schools in the Denver Public Schools region. She is also one of the co-founders of the hugely influential #DisruptTexts movement, whose mission is as follows:

> *#Disrupt Texts is a crowdsourced, grass roots effort by teachers for teachers to challenge the traditional canon in order to create a more inclusive, representative, and equitable language arts curriculum that our students deserve. It is part of our mission to aid and develop teachers committed to anti-racist/anti-bias teaching pedagogy and practices.*[28]

Torres says she sees her work with #DisruptTexts as being directly tied to increasing book access. "I feel that often the books folks have access to are books that have stood the test of time and been sanctioned by those in higher education," she tells me. "#DisruptTexts in the librarian world often looks like increasing access and inclusion in school libraries and curriculum for books that are written by #OwnVoices authors and may have been recently published. These are books that may not have passed the standards for what secondary education students should read that come from those within higher education, but many of them have won prestigious awards, such as the National Book Award, for example."

If you're unfamiliar with #OwnVoices, a 2018 article in *School Library Journal* notes that #OwnVoices is "a term credited to author Corinne Duyvis, who suggested the hashtag on Twitter in 2015 to 'recommend kidlit about diverse characters written by authors from that same diverse group.'"[29] Increasing diversity in publishing with this intention helps provide young readers with books that authentically represent the

28   https://disrupttexts.org/lets-get-to-work
29   Yorio, K. (2018) "#OwnVoices not familiar to all," *School Library Journal*, www.slj.com/ownvoices-not-familiar-all

characters they're reading about. Therefore, the #OwnVoices movement works to increase access to books that can be authentic mirrors for many of our students. In *Brightly*, an online magazine and literacy resource owned by Penguin Random House, Kayla Whaley shares this helpful context:

> *There's a long history of majority-group authors (white, abled, straight, cisgender, male, etc.) writing outside their experience to tell diverse stories. Sometimes the characters and stories they create are wonderful! But many times, they're rife with stereotypes, tropes, and harmful portrayals. Time and again, marginalized people have seen their stories taken from them, misused, and published as authentic, while marginalized authors have had to jump hurdle after hurdle to be published themselves.*[30]

As Torres tells me, these initiatives — to #DisruptTexts and fill schools with #OwnVoices books — are essential ways of improving book access. And for her, they're initiatives rooted in the conversations and advocacy work that she has led for a long time.

"The initiatives I have led have all begun with panels or presentations I have done within school districts or other organizations," she says. "I have worked as a curriculum developer with PBS Education, Blueshift Education, and many other school districts across the country. I have also been invited to present at ALA [American Library Association], NCTE [National Council of Teachers of English], and Kweli's Color of Children's Literature Conference. I am a board member for Book Love Foundation and through their Summer Book Club I ran a series of interviews with authors, and was involved in coordinating an affinity group for educators of color participating in the book club. The common thread in all these experiences was that educators wanted change. They know that what schools have traditionally done for students hasn't been working so well and under the current conditions we are facing some pretty serious challenges. I feel that librarians are uniquely positioned to work with language arts educators to bridge the gap between what students want to read and what they are assigned to read in schools."

---

30   Whaley, K. "#OwnVoices: why we need diverse authors in children's literature," Brightly, www.readbrightly.com/why-we-need-diverse-authors-in-kids-ya-lit (accessed September 2021)

In working to bridge this gap, many school librarians create access to books that historically have not been available in schools. It's important work that requires much broader support throughout the education world. As Torres says, "I believe that librarians will only be able to improve access when people inside the educational community begin to advocate for and value librarians as more than people who check books in and out. We have inherited a system of education with its roots in colonialism. As such, I don't believe the democratization of education can happen without decolonization taking place first."

In the context of education, decolonization refers to what the teacher and instructional coach Terry Kawi describes as "begin[ning] to analyze how dominant ideology and white supremacy have shaped our individual beliefs and behaviors."[31] Torres stresses the importance of decolonization in creating school libraries and classroom libraries composed of books that kids actually want to read. "Improving book access for those in our most marginalized school environments is part of this decolonization process," she says. "Because often the books those students have access to are not the ones they choose to read, which greatly compromises their opportunity to engage and fall in love with reading."

Dr. Krista Welz is another school librarian working hard to improve access for students. Welz, who works at North Bergen High School in New Jersey and was a 2017 recipient of *Library Journal*'s prestigious Movers and Shakers Award, is passionate about providing students access to what they need in order to be successful. In fact, the profile for her Movers and Shakers Award notes that "she increased annual circulation in her first year, 2013, by 97 percent. She also updated the 1960s-era collection and upgraded the outdated PCs to new Chromebase computers."[32]

Welz tells me that today's school librarians are uniquely positioned to increase access to information and technology for students. "School librarians are in charge of the information literacy hub of the school,"

---

31   Kawi, T. (2020) "Decolonizing our classrooms starts with us," PBS Teachers Lounge/ PBS Education, www.pbs.org/education/blog/decolonizing-our-classrooms-starts-with-us

32   www.libraryjournal.com/?detailStory=krista-welz-movers-shakers-2017-educators

she says. "They provide access to a multitude of print and digital reading material, as well as teach both students and teachers about the latest educational technology tools."

This role of teaching teachers about technology trends and tools is a relatively new and important one for school librarians. As we teach digital and technology literacy skills to teachers, we expand our reach as educators and help to increase access through greater understanding of *how* and *where* information can be found. Welz has worked hard to expand her reach even beyond her own school. "I offer my school district professional development sessions on Google Apps — or G Suite for Education — and other educational technology tools during school hours throughout the year," she says. "I also offer a course sponsored by my board of education and local teacher's union that enables me to teach teachers about the latest instructional methods in virtual and hybrid learning." This expansive role, she notes, is what the job of school librarian has become, and it has allowed her to continuously expand her skills and therefore become a leader in her school district and beyond.

Regarding the democratization of education, Welz points out that technology is what allows us to come closer to achieving that vision. "To me," she says, "democratizing education really means easy access to information for anyone, students and teachers alike. Teachers can teach a lesson and back it up with supplemental online material — such as YouTube — to further reinforce concepts. They can direct students who need more challenging content to other courses taught online by other teachers, like those available through Coursera. Sometimes students are bored with their school's curriculum and want to learn things on their own that spark their interest. And this is OK! With the use of personalized adaptive learning, such as Edmentum and Edgenuity, students can easily move on to other levels of assessment."

Welz feels strongly that giving students access to content that meets their particular needs — and teaching them how to navigate that content — is a crucial part of increasing access. She encourages educators to move beyond traditional notions of access to information. "The days of purchasing textbooks are over," she says. "They simply get outdated too quickly, and schools now have the option of going with open educational resources. There are many free textbooks online that teachers can now utilize in their classrooms, such as those from CK-12."

Welz also encourages educators to find or create online professional learning networks beyond their particular schools, as these networks can go a long way in helping us stay up to date with new and innovative ways to access books, information, and technology. "It was through Twitter that I found many opportunities in education," Welz says. She co-founded Edcamp Urban, an "unconference" in which participants — primarily from urban schools — are welcome to move freely from session to session and share their ideas and expertise in sessions that are spontaneously created on the day of the event. Indeed, the professional growth that comes with online networking is fundamental in helping all educators learn exactly how they can work to increase access for students.

Given the role of technology in granting students access to information, teaching specific technology skills has become an essential part of the school librarian's role. Therefore, school librarians must have opportunities and/or daily schedules that allow them to teach students and faculty alike — and therefore to be leaders in this area of education.

"Teachers need to see examples of how to use educational technology in classroom instruction," Welz tells me. "Either librarians can create instructional videos for teachers to watch or allow teachers to come into the library and watch them teach a lesson. Many schools are utilizing the Pineapple Chart method, an informal observation system where teachers go into other teachers' rooms to watch them teach a lesson. School librarians on a flex schedule can be really beneficial in this regard. Whether they co-teach with another teacher or bring in a class to model a lesson for a teacher, it's always a win-win. This is why I am such an advocate for the flex schedule for school librarians. High school librarians are more lucky in this sense. If elementary [and middle] schools allowed their school librarians to work on a flex schedule, instead of a fixed one, things would be a lot different."

Takeaways for all educators

For any educators interested in working to increase access to books, information, and technology, it's important to know that even seemingly small steps can make a big impact. And there are many ways to begin.

If you're a teacher interested in increasing book access, then starting, updating, or expanding your classroom library is a great place to begin. I would argue that all K-12 classrooms should have libraries of books — yes, even non-humanities high school classrooms. You don't have to have fiction. There are so many nonfiction books written specifically for young adults right now, and by providing your students with access to them you'll give them opportunities to dig deeper into the content you teach. You can sort books into bins by topic or genre. You can make sure books you think students will be particularly excited about have their covers facing forward for greater visibility. At the beginning of a class period, you might even read out the first page of a book to which you want to draw students' attention.

Whenever you have an upcoming project that would benefit from students having access to more books, move your class to the library for as many periods as you can. This is such an easy way to increase book access for your students and, speaking for many librarians, this option isn't taken advantage of nearly enough. If needed, we can show you and your students where books relevant to the project are located. In the next section, I'll explain how we can be of even greater service to you and your students in this kind of situation.

If you're a teacher looking to increase information and technology access, you can get started by taking a look at your curriculum and determining where it would be helpful for your students to have access to more information about any given topic: differing perspectives, audio or video instead of text, etc. You can do your own digging, obviously, but keep in mind that school librarians are information professionals and we can help you efficiently find pertinent, high-quality information. Then, once you've determined specifically what kind of information you'd like to provide, you can consult with your librarian and/or technology specialist to decide which digital tools or technologies would give your students the best access to that information. This could look like anything from linking to new resources on your class website (or online classroom management system) to beginning the process of securing new technology for your classroom or department.

If you're an administrator looking to increase book access, consider the ways that you show your school community you're a reader and books are important to you. After all, in order for the community to want to increase book access, a love for books has to be woven into the culture of your school. If you don't already, keep your own mini-library of education-related books in your office, with the book you're reading at any given time on your desk for teachers and students to see. Share passages that are relevant — or just passages that resonate with you — during faculty meetings. Read books that are popular with your students, too, and talk about them. And, of course, do everything you possibly can to secure adequate budgets for your school library and classroom libraries.

If you're an administrator looking to increase access to information and technology in your school, consider starting a committee tasked with exploring how information is accessed and used in your school — and to what effect. Where and how might students benefit from access to more information? What technology do they need in order to access that information?

In *Harnessing Technology for Deeper Learning*, Scott McLeod and Julie Graber provide helpful framing for this line of inquiry:

> *When educators use digital technologies for learning and teaching, those uses should be intentional and targeted. Educators should be able to clearly articulate what technology infusion is intended to accomplish for them and their students. In other words, as thoughtful users of learning technologies, we all should continually ask the question, 'Technology for the purpose of what?'*[33]

Once it's determined what technologies are needed and why, you can begin working to secure those technologies for your school. The number of digital and technological options available is overwhelming, and many of them won't actually benefit your particular school population. It's crucial to be as intentional as possible when considering how to increase access to information and technology for your community.

---

33   McLeod, S. & Graber, J. (2018) *Harnessing Technology for Deeper Learning*, Solution Tree

How your school librarian can help

Teachers, you don't have to work to increase access on your own. Your school librarian can and will support you. Here are some of the ways we can help.

- **Research interviews.** School librarians can schedule short meetings with individual students — or small groups — during which they help students clarify specifically what information they're looking for, identify which information resources (books, e-books, websites, databases, etc.) would be most helpful to check, and give advice on searching for information efficiently. Research interviews help in being intentional about *how* access is increased.

- **Curation.** Over the years, I've created many online guides for faculty and students in which I've curated links to information that meet their specific needs. School librarians are made for this work, and it's such an easy way to increase access to books and information for students. A significant part of this is creating access to information that offers alternative viewpoints and/or diverse perspectives. For example, if you're an English teacher who's required to teach *Lord of the Flies* but you have some reservations about the world view it espouses, you could ask your school librarian to help you collate additional resources that can help students see the text through a #DisruptTexts lens. Tricia Ebarvia, a co-founder of #DisruptTexts, provides examples of questions that could be considered during this process:

  - "How are characters portrayed and positioned?"
  - "Whose point of view is centered in this story?"
  - "Whose points of view are marginalized?"
  - "Which perspectives are missing?"[34]

- **Mini lessons.** We are happy to visit your classroom — or have you and your class visit the library — to teach students research

---

34   Ebarvia, T. (2018) "Disrupting texts as a restorative practice," https://triciaebarvia. org/2018/07/11/disrupting-texts-as-a-restorative-practice

or technology skills that are applicable to any given lesson, unit, or project. As I mentioned earlier, a big part of increasing access is helping students understand *how to find* the information they need. And given the sheer volume of information available online, teaching students this skill couldn't be more important right now. As John Palfrey writes in *BiblioTech*, "[librarians] are naturals when it comes to teaching young people to understand information quality."[35]

- **Consultations about classroom libraries.** Given our expertise, we can help you decide which books to order. We're up to date with book trends, reviews, and which voices most need amplifying, so we can help you build diverse collections that your students will love. We can also help you figure out how to best organize and display books within your classroom space, and even how to establish a mini borrowing system, if you'd like.

- **Advocacy.** School librarians want to help you provide your students with access to the books, information, and technology they need. If we can't provide this access ourselves, we can advocate for you. We will do everything we can to help. After all, increasing access is in our job description. All you have to do is ask.

Administrators, given the services we offer that you see above, you can invite us to pitch them — and have other faculty members share testimonials — on a regular basis during faculty meetings. Faculty familiarity with library services can increase access for your students. For the same reason, you might also consider asking us to lead faculty professional development sessions that help teachers learn about new apps or helpful digital tools. If a grant application needs to be written for more books or technology and you need some research (anecdotal and/or hard data) to support that appeal, we can help with that as well. We want to partner with you to help give students and faculty the resources they want and need.

---

35   Palfrey, J. (2015) *BiblioTech: Why Libraries Matter More Than Ever in the Age of Google*, Basic Books

Listening and responding

An underlying theme of this chapter — sometimes discussed explicitly, sometimes inferred — is that there are vast differences in student access from school to school. Collectively, we have not done what is necessary to democratize education. In the face of this injustice, educators in all schools have a very reliable source of wisdom that often goes untapped: our students. In *We Got This*, Cornelius Minor writes that our "superpower" as teachers is listening to our students and then responding accordingly. With this in mind, both sets of guiding questions below begin by encouraging you to talk to your students.[36]

Teachers:

- What kinds of books, information, and/or technology have your students told you they need or want to access? What is the first step you can take toward providing that access for them?

- What specific skills can you teach your students to help them become less reliant on educators in finding the resources they need? Have you asked your students this question?

- Do you have a classroom library? If so, how could it be diversified and/or expanded? If not, what is the first step you can take toward creating one? What books have your students told you they like to read?

- Are your students aware of all the resources available through the school library? If not, how can you work with your school librarian to increase their awareness?

Administrators:

- How are you creating space for direct dialogue with your students about what they need from the school? How can increasing access to books, information, and technology help provide them with what they need? What is the first step you can take toward increasing access to what they need?

- Is your school library fully funded? If not, what is the first step you can take to make this happen as soon as possible?

36   Minor, C. (2018) *We Got This: Equity, Access, and the Quest to Be Who Our Students Need Us to Be*, Heinemann Educational Books

- Do you provide time during faculty meetings for your school librarian to teach the faculty about book, information, and technology access? Do your students have regular and consistent access to the librarian? Does the librarian's schedule allow for this?

- Do most classrooms in your school have libraries of relevant books? If not, what is the first step you can take toward jumpstarting the creation of these libraries throughout the school? How can your school librarian help?

Chapter 3

Centering inclusivity

"To love all children, we must struggle together to create the schools we are taught to believe are impossible: Schools built on justice, love, joy, and anti-racism"

— Bettina L. Love

On my father's side, I'm a first-generation American. My father spent his first seven years growing up in Tehran, Iran, and then his family moved across the world to Salt Lake City — thankfully well before the violence of the Iranian Revolution.

Upon arrival in the US, his parents shifted the language spoken at home to all English, all the time. Their reason for this, like many American immigrant parents over the generations, was to "Americanize" their family as much as possible. I completely understand their rationale for doing so. There was pressure to adapt, and they wanted their children to adjust well to their new home.

Historically speaking, US schools have been a primary source of that pressure. Rather than accommodating — much less appreciating — a plurality of identities, our schools have largely ignored, silenced, and denigrated anything that strays from straight, white, male, cisgendered, Christian, able-bodied, European American narratives. The loss of culture, and therefore loss of self-identity, among young people whose identities do not match this one has been nothing short of tragic. Our schools have by and large actively perpetuated a form of identity erasure. And although this erasure cannot be undone, there are plenty of ways that today's educators can make room for — and ideally amplify — the voices of those who have been marginalized for so long.

In the previous chapter, I discussed the school librarian's role within the school community as staunch protector of intellectual freedom. Part of advancing intellectual freedom is providing students with access to curricula and resources that give voice to diverse perspectives. After all, our students cannot truly be free if they do not see themselves, or at least essential parts of themselves, represented in the content taught by their teachers and in the books their schools make available to them.

Take the example of race, a critical component of identity. In the past, people who were not White had to go outside the traditional American education system to educate themselves in ways that honored who they were and, in many cases, to educate themselves period. For example, in *Cultivating Genius*, the literacy scholar Gholdy Muhammad shares an entire equity framework she has created, rooted in the extraordinary work of African American literary societies in the early 1800s. As Muhammad puts it, these societies "were essentially collaborative teaching and learning spaces to construct knowledge and engage one another toward cultivating a literary culture."[37]

That definition is striking to me for two reasons. First, it describes the kind of space that today's school librarians seek to create. Second, this work itself — creating an intellectual space that is comfortable for those who have been historically marginalized — is clearly not new or innovative.

I've learned through speaking to literacy experts in the process of writing this book that it's important to keep this second point in mind as we schools consider how to move forward with centering inclusivity. In many ways, school librarians are finally catching up to the extraordinary

---

37   Muhammad, G. (2020) *Cultivating Genius: An Equity Framework for Culturally and Historically Responsive Literacy*, Scholastic

educational efforts of BIPOC (Black, Indigenous, and people of color) educators and parents of the past — efforts that, out of necessity, had to happen outside school.

The work itself may not be new. However, today's school librarians can be — and often are — innovative in the way we center inclusivity within our school communities. That's what this chapter is about.

First, I'll define inclusivity and anti-racism (a crucial element of inclusivity) specifically within the context of schools. I'll also discuss some of the pushback you're likely to encounter when working to center inclusivity within your school and some suggestions on how to work through it.

In the sections that follow I'll share how school librarians are leading efforts to center inclusivity in schools. I'll detail some of the work I've done in my school to center inclusivity and give examples from innovative school librarians throughout the US. Finally, I'll share suggested takeaways for all educators and how you can work with your school librarian to center inclusivity in your classroom, school, and/or district.

Inclusivity

Many educators use the word inclusion to refer to the act of bringing students who need additional support — usually referred to as special education — into so-called general education classes and experiences. With no intention of diminishing that practice, in this chapter I discuss inclusion in a much broader context.

For this reason, I have chosen to use the word inclusivity, rather than inclusion, because I believe it speaks more directly to what I'm talking about. When I discuss inclusivity I'm referring to the practice of centering the voices and needs of those who have been historically marginalized.

As I mentioned earlier, the favored perspective in American schools has long been that of the straight, white, male, Christian, able-bodied, European American. When we center inclusivity in schools, we draw together a diversity of perspectives — a diversity of identities — into our educational practice. This is important work that helps us democratize education. It's work that helps us honor all our students for who they are and what they have to offer.

When we talk about inclusivity, it's important to keep in mind that the vast majority of teachers in the US are White: almost 80% of public school teachers and 85% of independent school teachers.[38] This lack of racial diversity is important context to consider when working toward inclusivity in schools. When the vast majority of teachers are White, it's all too easy to perpetuate White-centric narratives. The work of centering inclusivity, therefore, is that much more difficult and that much more urgent.

Anti-racism

Anti-racism is an incredibly important element of inclusivity. For clarity's sake, it's important to define anti-racism and what exactly it means to be an anti-racist. Decidedly different from "not being racist," anti-racism requires action and movement. It requires doing.

In the very beginning of *How to be an Antiracist*, Dr. Ibram X. Kendi defines an anti-racist as a person "who is supporting an antiracist policy through their actions or expressing an antiracist idea."[39] Another helpful definition comes from *This Book is Anti-Racist*, written for middle and high school students, in which Tiffany Jewell defines anti-racism in this way:

> *Anti-racism is actively working against racism. It is making a commitment to resisting unjust laws, policies, and racist attitudes. Anti-racism is how we get free from centuries of living in a racialized society that keeps us separate and oppressed.*[40]

With these definitions in mind, we can reflect on the ways in which our actions as educators are or are not anti-racist — and how we can do more of the former. After all, anti-racism in education is directly connected to other ways of centering inclusivity in schools. In an article, the Learning for Justice (formerly Teaching Tolerance) board member Jamilah Pitts explains this important connection: "Anti-racist educators understand that all forms of oppression are connected, that it is not possible to care

38   https://nces.ed.gov/fastfacts/display.asp?id=28
39   Kendi, I.X. (2019) *How to Be an Antiracist*, Random House
40   Jewell, T. (2020) *This Book is Anti-Racist*, Frances Lincoln

about racism and disregard the violence in sexism, classism, homophobia and more."[41]

Advancing our school's anti-racist efforts is an important way that school librarians work to center inclusivity. We'll take a look at how, but first let's consider some of the pushback you might encounter in your efforts to center inclusivity in your school.

Responding to pushback

One would think K-12 educators would be well beyond the point of having to justify any action that centers inclusivity in our schools. Our job is to serve our students — every single one of them. The sad truth is that we are not beyond the need to justify centering inclusivity. If you already do this work in your school, chances are you've encountered some pushback. If you haven't already, you will.

The level of pushback will differ from school to school, depending in large part on the culture of your school community. But you will encounter at least some pushback, and it's important to think about where it's coming from and how to respond. Your actions can change the culture of your school for the better.

Below, I've included a few (certainly not all) examples of pushback and some recommendations for how you can respond.

Tradition

In the school setting, tradition refers to the ways in which ideologies, practices, approaches, and even texts have been passed down from one generation to the next. Traditions can be important and beneficial, to be sure. But when they inhibit or prohibit a school from centering inclusivity, they're problematic. Some educators defend problematic traditions in schools, such as singing songs at school assemblies with racist undertones or overtones, by saying some version of a statement like "This is the way we've always done things," a frustrating position that is clearly devoid of critical thought. You might also hear some version of "If it's not broken, don't fix it." This is a particularly problematic argument because it indicates that the person is unaware that what you're talking

---

41   Pitts, J. (2020) "What anti-racism really means for educators," Learning for Justice, www.learningforjustice.org/magazine/what-antiracism-really-means-for-educators

about is indeed broken. To address problematic traditions, you can find and present research to support your position, which is really not hard to find when it comes to the positive effects of centering inclusivity. The Civil Rights Project from the University of California, Los Angeles, is a great place to start.[42] You can even tap your school librarian to help you find and/or curate research, which can then be shared with the appropriate department head, administrator, or even superintendent.

Complacency

This can be directly connected to tradition, of course, because sometimes by following traditions we become complacent. Regardless of how or why it happens, sometimes educators become complacent without even realizing that they have. They're satisfied with what they're doing and/ or see no reason to do things differently. Complacency is an enemy of progress, and in order to center inclusivity in our schools we must do what we can to disrupt it. This doesn't mean we have to start battles within our departments or within our schools. Sometimes fresh ideas, especially with the stated intention of making classrooms and/or the school more inclusive for all students, can be enough to inspire complacent educators to shake things up. If there's resistance, being patient and speaking with enthusiasm about your idea can go a long way toward building understanding — and ultimately support — for your cause.

Discomfort

Sometimes centering inclusivity can be uncomfortable for educators. Whether it's because they're new and afraid of sharing ideas or because they fear what might happen if they attempt to make a change, discomfort can lead to pushback. Perhaps you or a colleague fall into this camp. If so, keep in mind that when it comes to centering inclusivity, silence is complicity. Inaction is complicity. And we are all capable of doing difficult things. Temporary discomfort with disrupting the status quo is worth the positive effects for students, especially those who have been marginalized.

Racism

To put it plainly, racism exists everywhere. It's in you, it's in me — explored or unexplored. Therefore, your school is not immune and

---

42   www.civilrightsproject.ucla.edu/research/k-12-education/integration-and-diversity

neither is mine. Racist language, actions, or policies harm young people — the very people we are tasked with serving. The question is what we can do about it. In an article for Learning for Justice, Brian Willoughby shares the following questions from Mica Pollock, editor of the book *Everyday Antiracism*,[43] to help you determine the prevalence of racism within your school and how to begin to address it.

- "Am I seeing, understanding and addressing the ways the world treats me and my students as members of racial groups?"
- "Am I seeing, understanding and addressing communities and individuals in their full complexity?"
- "Am I seeing, understanding and addressing the ways opportunities to learn or thrive are unequally distributed to racial groups?"
- "What actions offer necessary opportunities to students in such a world?"
- "Is this action moving students closer to educational opportunity or farther away from it? Why? What is our evidence?"[44]

Accusations of "radical agenda"

This kind of pushback is politically motivated, of course, and comes most often from parents. But, perhaps more disturbingly, it can also come internally from educators. It's not a form of pushback that most schools have to deal with, but it certainly exists and therefore it's worth discussing here. The reality we're all faced with is one in which centering all voices and perspectives is seen by some as a ploy to diminish White people. For example, take the sentiment shared by the former Secretary of State, Mike Pompeo. On his last day in the job in January 2021, he tweeted that multiculturalism is "not who America is."[45] The promotion of this ideology by one of our country's highest offices is a reminder

43   Pollock, M. (ed). (2008) *Everyday Antiracism: Getting Real About Race in School*, The New Press

44   Willoughby, B. (2013) "Is my school racist?", Learning for Justice, www.learningforjustice.org/magazine/fall-2013/is-my-school-racist

45   Hansler, J., Atwood, K. & Gaouette, N. (2021) "Pompeo attacks multiculturalism, saying it is 'not who America is,'" CNN, www.cnn.com/2021/01/19/politics/pompeo-multiculturalism-tweet/index.html

of how much work we still have to do. We must be bold and direct in our response to any such claims. As educators, we are responsible for honoring the voices and talents of all our students. And we must be extra-mindful of those students who, because of some aspect of their identities, have been ignored, silenced, or otherwise harmed by schools and/or society. This important work transcends partisan politics. And if this work is dubbed "radical" or "liberal" by colleagues or constituents, we must be truth-tellers who share without hesitation that if we're believers in democracy — in the equality and importance of all voices — then we must democratize education.

School libraries leading the way

Cornelius Minor, the literacy expert and author referenced at the end of the previous chapter, tells me that of all the educators he has had throughout his life, the one who had the greatest impact was his high school librarian. In fact, Minor says she saved his life.

"I was an angry high school student," he explains. "I was one of 10 Black kids at my school, and White parents actively opposed my presence." In the face of this racism, Minor's high school librarian helped by connecting him with books such as *The Fire Next Time* by James Baldwin. Through conversation and book recommendations, she became a mentor and hugely influential person in his life. He still talks to her every week.

Not all high school graduates go on to talk to their high school librarian every week, of course, but Minor's story points to the important role that school librarians play in young people's lives. By taking an active interest in their interests and reading habits, we're able to recommend books to students that can help them better understand themselves and each other. It's a role that really does have a great impact.

This is why we care so much about centering inclusivity. We know that our book collections must be of interest to *all* our students. Therefore, our leadership in centering inclusivity in our schools begins largely with the transformative act of growing and maintaining libraries of diverse and contemporary books — and then getting these books into the hands of as many students as possible. School librarians network with other school librarians about trends, read the latest literature on books for young people, and constantly weed out books that are outdated. As Pat Scales writes in *School Library Journal*, the library "serves all patrons: all cultures, races, genders, sexual orientation and identification."[46] Accordingly, we focus on building collections that allow all students to find crucial aspects of themselves represented in the stories made available to them. Scales shares why certain books are withdrawn from our collections:

> *Nonfiction becomes quickly outdated, especially in science and social studies, and titles with inaccurate information should be removed. Books considered 'classics' often reflect stereotypes that are unacceptable in children's books today. These must be reevaluated for insensitive stereotypes. Children aren't yet discerning learners or readers. They must be given accurate information and books free of stereotypes that could damage their views of other cultures, races, or themselves.*[47]

This is the critical eye that we bring to maintaining contemporary, diverse book collections within the school library. And we bring this same critical eye to conversations with our colleagues — teachers and administrators — about the books taught in classrooms throughout the school. We know what's most recommended by critics and other educators, and we know what students enjoy reading. We're always eager to connect students with books they will love. This is, of course, one of the oldest roles of the school librarian and it remains one of the most important.

As illustrated by Minor's story about his high school librarian, sharing the right book with the right young person can have an incredibly positive impact on that young person's sense of self. In this way, school librarians have great power. And we do our best to exercise this power responsibly and as often as possible.

In my own work as a school librarian, I work hard to diversify our book catalog. I approach this work as a never-ending process. I also make sure

---

46   Scales, S. (2021) "Virtual story time challenges; objection to books on immigration | Scales on censorship," *School Library Journal*, www.slj.com/virtual-story-time-challenges-objection-to-books-on-immigration-scales-on-censorship

47   Ibid.

the books I display and talk about with students and teachers — from nonfiction picture books to graphic novels — are representative of this diversity. We can't just have new, diverse books on our shelves. Visibility and awareness matter, too. When students and faculty see the library spotlighting books that represent a variety of voices and perspectives, the school itself feels like — and indeed becomes — a safer, more inclusive community.

Whenever a new book arrives and I know it might be a good option for a particular grade level or subject, I check it out to the appropriate teacher and bring it directly to them. If they're not in their classroom or at their desk, I leave it with a sticky note briefly explaining why I thought it might be of interest. Sometimes these books even become part of the teachers' curricula. Small gestures can have a big impact.

I also provide teachers with specific resources — articles, books, websites, etc. — that not only help their students dive more deeply into a particular topic of study, but also diversify the perspectives on the topic. I have found that problematizing commonly held understandings or interpretations is an important way that we as educators can center inclusivity.

By opening new doors for students, we let in more light. Students come to see their topic of study more clearly and more fully. And over time, with repeated exposure to a diversity of perspectives, they come to see that the world isn't just this way or that way. They learn to question dominant narratives, thereby greatly increasing their critical thinking skills.

School librarians are also teachers themselves, of course. In my own teaching, centering inclusivity usually begins with reflecting on my pedagogical approach. I see this reflection as akin to the concept of "beginner's mind" in Zen Buddhism, which asks us to drop all preconceptions of the topic, matter, or person at hand — to see whatever it is with fresh eyes. For me, this kind of reflection often involves stepping back and asking myself questions about why I'm teaching what I'm teaching, as well as questions about what my students need from me and library programming in general. In turn, this questioning has led me to design curricula that allow all my students space to explore their unique interests, backgrounds, and passions.

This choice-based approach to teaching and learning is rooted in ongoing and meaningful professional development, which has been the primary way that I try to maintain something close to the beginner's mind as a teacher. From the years I spent participating in the National SEED (Seeking Educational Equity and Diversity) Project to engaging with inspiring ABAR (anti-bias, anti-racist) educators on Twitter, a common theme in my learning about centering inclusivity has been the importance of giving students choice. When I give my students choice in what they read and how they can show what they know, I find they are often much more engaged, there are significantly fewer classroom management issues, and, most important of all, they often learn more about themselves through their own unique interests.

My emphasis on choice begins with the youngest students I teach: second graders. Inspired by other school librarians, for library class each week I set up different learning stations. Each station has a different activity or game, and students move freely from one station to the next. The only requirements are that they visit at least two different stations in each class period and they don't stay too long at one station if it's full and other students are waiting to join.

I use subjects or topics they're learning about in the classroom as springboards for the kinds of stations I design, while also making sure the stations help them learn and practice foundational library skills, especially those prioritized by the American Association of School Librarians Framework for Learners: inquiry, inclusion, collaboration, curation, exploration, and engagement.[48] The stations rotate from week to week.

What I love about giving students choice is that it avoids a one-size-fits-all approach to learning. It gives students opportunities to ask questions or dig into content that I might not have thought about beforehand. It creates space for my students to explore their own unique interests and even parts of their identities that the school hasn't given them room to explore before.

---

48   American Association of School Librarians. (2018) *AASL Standards Framework for Learners*, American Library Association. https://standards.aasl.org/wp-content/uploads/2017/11/AASL-Standards-Framework-for-Learners-pamphlet.pdf

One particular example that comes to mind is when a Jewish student of mine spent a school year learning and writing about Israel as part of the Passion Project I co-facilitate for our fifth-grade students (I discuss this project in Chapter 1). This student had voiced that parts of his experience at our school had been painful owing to a lack of inclusivity around his religion — everything from which holidays are observed or respected to the content of winter assemblies. He appreciated the opportunity to do a deep dive into Israel and his Jewish identity and ultimately, as the culmination of the project, to share what he had learned with our school community. Giving him choice helped him feel seen and, by extension, included.

Forward-thinking librarians

School librarians work with students and teachers across grades and disciplines, and we are specially attuned to issues of access and equity, so we generally have a good sense of where and how there's a lack of inclusivity in our schools. When I was taking graduate classes toward my school librarian certification, the first high school librarian I visited for an observation showed me, on a whim, the library study room that was home to the school's popular GSA (Gay-Straight Alliance). She mentioned that she had worked with students to make that group a reality because there had not been one before, and it was a space that was much needed in their school community. This is the kind of grassroots work that school librarians often lead. We see a need and we do what we can to address it.

Take Peter Langella, a librarian at Champlain Valley Union High School in Hinesburg, Vermont, who was horrified when the school library "was the target of racist and anti-Semitic writing, drawing, and graffiti."[49] In his article for *Knowledge Quest*, Langella shares how he worked with several colleagues to spearhead the following four initiatives:

1. A faculty book study of Robin DiAngelo's *White Fragility*.
2. A series of talks about power and privilege for the entire community, with Langella's stated goal of providing "consistent time and space to normalize conversations among students about social issues

---

49   Langella, P. (2019) "Diversity and inclusion in libraries: more than books on the shelves," *Knowledge Quest*, https://knowledgequest.aasl.org/diversity-and-inclusion-in-libraries-more-than-books-on-the-shelves

and to cultivate equity, diversity, and inclusion within the school community."

3. In conjunction with local public libraries, a summer reading project centered around *March: Book One*, the popular graphic novel about the civil rights leader and US congressman John Lewis.

4. A newly designed elective, taught by Langella, "that uses theme- and choice-based reading assignments to teach and cultivate empathy."

Leadership initiatives such as these illustrate how librarians show up and step up for our students. Given our skillset and direct connection to the student body as a whole, school librarians are uniquely positioned to make a positive, large-scale difference in our schools. And centering inclusivity is a matter of necessity. Langella concludes his article by emphasizing the urgency with which librarians must act to prevent students from feeling unheard, unseen, or, worst of all, unsafe:

> *Students in our schools are clamoring for more relevant and relatable school curriculum, and they're clamoring for their educators to better understand their lived experiences. We can't afford to wait until they walk through our library doors to find a book on the shelf. We must force the issue because the curriculum and practices and systems and structures will not shift fast enough without our direct action.*[50]

For school librarians, our purview extends beyond having the right books on our bookshelves. It's about being innovative in the way we center inclusivity in our curricula and the corresponding initiatives that we launch within our schools.

Another great example of a school librarian leading the way when it comes to inclusivity is Cicely Lewis, librarian at Meadowcreek High School in Norcross, Georgia. Lewis was named the 2020 School Librarian of the Year by *School Library Journal* for the impressive work she has done to center inclusivity — particularly anti-racism — through her school library programming. Lewis started the popular Read Woke initiative after her students voiced their fear and concerns about police violence against Black people.

---

50   Ibid.

In an article in *School Library Journal*, Lewis explains that the Read Woke initiative calls for students — and teachers — to read a set number of books that:

- "Challenge a social norm."
- "Give voice to the voiceless."
- "Provide information about a group that has been disenfranchised."
- "Seek to challenge the status quo."
- "Have a protagonist from an underrepresented or oppressed group."[51]

Once participants confirm that they've read their books, Lewis awards them a Read Woke T-shirt, which is a badge of honor for the recipients. On her website, Lewis notes that those who finish the reading challenge also have their picture added to the school's Read Woke wall and receive a free book. "Our circulation has increased as a result, and we even have teachers onboard who have earned shirts," she writes on her blog.[52]

The idea has spread. As Wayne D'Orio explains in his profile of Lewis for her School Librarian of the Year award, the initiative has become a full-fledged movement:

> *[The] Read Woke movement is an international phenomenon among educators. The idea behind it — reading books to arm yourself with knowledge to better protect your rights, give voice to the voiceless, and challenge social norms — is wildly popular. The program was named the American Library Association's best literature program for teens in 2019, and Lewis won the National Teacher Award for Lifelong Readers that same year. Read Woke groups have popped up in Norway and Canada.[53]*

---

51   Lewis, C. (2018) "'Read Woke' school reading challenge makes an impact," *School Library Journal*, www.slj.com/read-woke-school-reading-challenge-makes-impact

52   Lewis, C. (2017) "#ReadWoke," https://cicelythegreat.wordpress.com/2017/11/20/readwoke

53   D'Orio, W. (2020) "'Reading is my superpower': Cicely Lewis, 2020 School Librarian of the Year," *School Library Journal*, www.slj.com/?detailStory=Reading-is-my-superpower-Cicely-Lewis-2020-School-Librarian-of-the-Year-Books-libraries

The forward-thinking work that school librarians do to center inclusivity in our schools involves listening to our students, responding to their diverse needs, and constantly asking ourselves how we can better meet those needs. It's the kind of work that never ends.

Maegen Rose, middle school librarian at Rye Country Day School in Rye, New York, stresses that school librarians can't opt out of this work, even when it doesn't feel urgent in some school communities. In my conversation with Rose, she emphasizes how this work begins with being intentional about the kinds of book collections that librarians build, the books we display, and how we talk about these books with students and teachers. She notes that there's always the possibility that inclusivity and anti-racist initiatives can be conflated with progressive politics. "Because of this," she says, "I do this work with extra vigilance and extra care."

Rose loves #OwnVoices books and she makes it a point to publicize which she is reading at any given time. Whenever she's teaching — with others or in her own lessons on information literacy — she tries to normalize for students and faculty the voices, perspectives, and needs of people of color. "As librarians, we're so uniquely embedded in our schools," she says. "We have the benefit of seeing students and teachers across divisions and grade levels. And we're the information professionals. We have to be leaders in this work."

Takeaways for all educators

If you're a teacher or administrator who feels compelled to center inclusivity in new ways or perhaps with more urgency than before, I hope the examples in the previous section will provide inspiration and motivation. Now, let's explore more specifically how you might begin today.

Teachers, I suggest you start by applying "beginner's mind" to what you're teaching and how you're teaching it. This really does require you to see your work from a distance, as if you're looking down at it from the clouds with nothing but curiosity. This way, you can reflect on your practice with more objectivity. You can be more discerning in thinking about what your students need from you, from the class(es) you teach, and from school in general. This leads to questioning your own rationale for the specific content you teach and perhaps even beginning to trace where that rationale comes from. If you sit and start this gentle self-inventory, whether through silent reflection or journaling, you begin to see opportunities. And any opportunity to center inclusivity is worth taking advantage of.

When you find yourself reflecting on your curricula, I recommend you sharpen your focus on where you have and have not allowed space for students to choose their topics of study, the books they read, or the ways in which they show their learning. Wherever you have not allowed space for student choice, consider the potential impact of doing so: when we give students choices, we honor their voices. In an article for Edutopia, the humanities teacher Joshua Block helps clarify the many options we have for giving students choice, as well as the connection between choice and voice:

> There are times when students are able to pursue their passions and independently create projects, and other times when students can be given choice in smaller, yet meaningful, ways. The parameters of choice vary depending on the cycles of the school year, the specific students, the project, and many other factors. Regardless of the scenario, maintaining a focus on student choice helps to create learning environments of meaning where student voices matter.[54]

Any opportunities you provide for your students to choose will allow for greater inclusivity in your classroom. Students come to feel more in control of their own learning and, just as importantly, they see that you value what they have to say. Choice goes a long way in creating a classroom culture of inclusivity — the feeling that everyone belongs.

If you're compelled to spark a larger movement within your school that has the potential to center inclusivity, consider asking students — as many as possible — what they are concerned or worried about. You might already know some of this information from hearing their conversations between classes or in the hallways. You may have your own

---

54   Block, J. (2014) "Student choice leads to student voice," *Edutopia*, www.edutopia. org/blog/student-choice-leads-to-voice-joshua-block

valuable ideas about how to center inclusivity in your community, but students' voices are just as valuable. They often frame things in ways that I hadn't considered before, thereby leading to a different, more complex understanding of a problem or issue.

Once you've identified a system problem(s) around inclusivity, you can connect with like-minded or trusted colleagues who can help you brainstorm ways to begin to address the problem(s). I find that no matter how great I think an idea is, it always becomes better, bigger, or clearer after I've talked it through with others. It's also unlikely that a systemic issue can be fixed by you working alone. Perhaps you'll end up creating some kind of new learning opportunity for students or teachers, such as a student elective or faculty book study. Or perhaps you'll end up leading some kind of larger initiative that involves both students and teachers. Regardless, you'll need collaborators and/or supporters — folks who will stand with you or behind you.

You'll also want to think about how you're going to make — and keep — your initiative visible to the school community. Anything from posters in the hallway to announcements or graphics on the school's social media accounts can help you grow awareness. Important questions to consider are how and where you'll pitch it, and how you can help as many students, teachers, and even parents as possible see what you're doing and why it's important. Most importantly, you'll want to consider how you can get student buy-in. You're doing this for them, after all. However you're centering inclusivity, you'll need to keep their voiced needs and concerns in mind.

Like the Read Woke initiative, if students are directly involved and see firsthand how your initiative benefits them, they'll be its biggest supporters. Channeling their innate creativity through direct participation in a cause gives them the opportunity to make a difference for themselves, their classmates, and the future of the school.

Administrators, if you're interested in doing more work to center inclusivity in your school, then I highly recommend that you begin by using the beginner's mind, too — particularly regarding school culture. With gentle curiosity, try to see your school's customs, traditions, values, and habits from an emotionally removed perspective. While the nature of your role means you're already accustomed to seeing your school through a wider lens, making space for new, ongoing reflection on how your school can better center inclusivity will ultimately make a big difference for students and teachers. In your role, centering inclusivity could take many forms, including but not limited to:

- Actively seeking diversity for leadership positions.
- During interviews with teaching candidates, asking specific questions about how they've centered inclusion or advanced anti-racism in the classroom — no matter their subject.
- Facilitating ongoing professional development that helps the school as a whole center inclusivity.
- Surveying faculty and students about how and where the school is missing the mark in terms of centering inclusivity.

Finally, it's always worthwhile to consider hiring an outside consultant who has a track record in helping schools center inclusivity. These professionals come preconfigured with the beginner's mind because they don't know your school, yet they have a lot of experience in working with other schools so will know what to look for and how to help.

Part of your job, of course, is to not only center inclusivity for students, but also to center inclusivity for your entire faculty. Therefore, consider where and how you allow the faculty to choose. For example, instead of choosing one all-faculty summer read, consider how providing multiple book options — and multiple corresponding book discussions in the fall — might allow faculty to feel a little more in control of their own professional learning.

Or, instead of planning a single on-site PD event, consider offering different workshops or presentation opportunities that faculty members are free to move between. You might even ask faculty to create mini-presentations for each other in which they share new and/or exciting things happening in their classrooms: lessons, projects, digital apps that are working well, etc. We've experimented with this kind of PD at our school. It shows everyone the incredible expertise within the school and honors the voices of teachers who otherwise might not be heard.

How your school librarian can help

Teachers, school librarians are passionate about centering inclusivity and we want to help you in any way possible. Below are a few specific examples of how we can assist.

- **Co-planning curriculum.** We're more than happy to talk through any ideas you might have about centering inclusivity in your curriculum. Much of how school librarians see content is through the lens of inclusivity, so we can be helpful partners in planning curricula that center the voices of marginalized people and/or problematize traditional narratives. We can point you directly to resources that offer new or different perspectives on the topic at hand, and then we can work with you to determine where exactly these resources fit with any plans you already have. We can also help you design activities that enable students to evaluate — and, with older students, synthesize — these new and/or different perspectives. We can help you develop lessons that teach students metacognitive strategies that make their unconscious bias conscious — for example, "Whose voice is *not* included here and probably should be?" This is closely linked to our work in teaching information literacy, which involves helping students learn how to effectively analyze information. In this case, we're talking about developing a more inclusive mindset when it comes to reading and interpreting, which is an essential part of effectively analyzing information.

- **Co-teaching.** I've been on both sides of this equation: I occasionally co-taught with a librarian when I was a classroom teacher and now, as a librarian, I regularly co-teach with classroom teachers. What better way to practice inclusivity than to include another educator in your teaching? And with the inclusivity-centric lens we bring to our work, inviting us to co-teach lessons with you — or, if our schedules allow, regular visits throughout a whole unit — can be especially helpful. Ideally we will have some lesson-planning conversations with you beforehand. But, either way, we're happy to be an active part of your classroom as you strive to center inclusivity in your teaching. In my experience, just having another leading voice in the classroom makes for a more dynamic classroom environment. And if you're both working together toward the common goal of centering inclusivity then positive change is just around the corner.

- **Co-leading.** If you're looking to lead some kind of inclusivity initiative that extends beyond your classroom, and you'd like some help getting that initiative off the ground, reach out to your school librarian. Creating a more inclusive culture for our schools is incredibly important to us and there are various ways that we can work with you to advance this cause. We can co-host inclusivity-centric events in the library, co-sponsor initiatives aiming to diversify required reading lists for students, co-launch committees seeking to advance anti-racist pedagogy throughout the school or district, and more. Just tell us what you have in mind. Given that we have access to students and teachers in multiple grade levels, we can help you extend your reach. Most importantly, we want to stand beside you in this work.

Administrators, whatever you have in mind in terms of centering inclusivity, it's absolutely worth connecting with your school librarian. Just like you, we serve students and teachers alike, which can be quite helpful when planning for actions to take that are school-wide in scope. We can point you in the right direction in terms of information resources that might be helpful. We can brainstorm ideas with you about how to engage more faculty members and more students in this work. In the library, we can host guest speakers and workshops. You can even ask us to share our expertise on contemporary books and book trends with the whole faculty, so the school can develop a shared commitment to honoring a diversity of voices and identities. And finally, I recommend including us on leadership teams where decisions are being made. We're committed to this work and we want to help you improve school culture in such a way that all students feel heard, seen, and understood.

Struggling together

Centering inclusivity is often difficult work, especially in the face of White supremacy that extends well beyond history books and fringe organizations. But educators are charged with caring for all the students we teach, so this is work that must be done — and we must do it together. Here are some guiding questions for teachers and administrators that can help you begin to move forward.

Teachers:

- Which voices are underrepresented in your curricula? What steps can you take right now to include and honor those voices? Have you asked your school librarian to help?

- What are the books or lessons you teach that have remained unchanged for many years? How might you make room for new, contemporary voices or perspectives? Have you asked your school librarian to help?

- How and where could you give students choice in what they study and how they show what they've learned?

- What kind of professional development would be most helpful for you in learning more about anti-racist teaching practices and ways to center inclusivity in schools?

Administrators:

- How do you model inclusivity in your leadership style with students? With teachers? With parents?

- How can you update the questions you ask teaching candidates to delve more into their proficiency with inclusive teaching practices?

- Does your faculty have ongoing conversations about centering inclusivity? If so, what could help these conversations lead to prompt action or positive change? If not, what can you do today to begin these conversations? Have you asked your school librarian to help?

- What kinds of forums — affinity groups, anonymous surveys, etc. — does your school provide for students whose voices or identities have historically been marginalized? If none, what can you do to create forums for students to share the ways in which they feel their voices are not being heard or are even ignored?

Chapter 4

Promoting and teaching multiple literacies

"Being a literate person today means more than being able to read and write"
— **Maureen Connolly and Vicky Giouroukakis**

Despite the wonderful evolution of school libraries over the years, there are still a lot of teachers, administrators, and parents who have an antiquated notion of what school librarians do. Many still believe that our job is to supervise the books in the library and shush all who enter — and that if we're elementary school librarians, all we do is host story time.

Perhaps for some of us, this is what our school librarians did back when we were students. Or perhaps this notion is based on the still-perpetuated media stereotype of librarians. Regardless of where this perception comes from, school librarianship is different now and has been for quite some time.

Although promoting a love of reading and teaching textual literacy are still essential parts of our job, it's time for the full scope of our work to be recognized and understood. Accordingly, the focus of this chapter is how, by and large, school librarians have come to teach not just one kind of literacy — textual literacy — but *multiple* literacies.

In addition to textual literacy, we teach visual literacy, information literacy, digital literacy, technological literacy, and racial literacy. There are other literacies, too, and they are all prioritized differently from school to school, but the literacies listed above are taught quite often by today's school librarians.

In 2019, the National Council of Teachers of English in the US shared the following statement, which provides helpful context for why our students need multiple literacies.

> *Literacy has always been a collection of communicative and sociocultural practices shared among communities. As society and technology change, so does literacy. The world demands that a literate person possess and intentionally apply a wide range of skills, competencies, and dispositions. These literacies are interconnected, dynamic, and malleable. As in the past, they are inextricably linked with histories, narratives, life possibilities, and social trajectories of all individuals and groups.*[55]

Twenty-first century school librarians are often tasked with leading the charge of teaching these multiple literacies. As you can imagine, this is no small task. But we care a lot about this work, because we know that being literate in each of these areas is vitally important for today's young people to be safe, successful, and knowledgeable. Right now, our students are faced with a whole host of challenges — from how to navigate our racialized world to how to be online — and school librarians are uniquely equipped and positioned within schools to help students address these challenges.

Promoting and teaching multiple literacies is a primary way in which we undertake this work. School librarians are expected to have expertise in textual, visual, digital, and technological literacy. Most of us do. And although I cannot claim that most school librarians teach racial literacy, a rapidly growing number of us prioritize this work. Given school librarians' extensive work in centering inclusivity, outlined in Chapter 3, many of us are school leaders — or well on our way to becoming school leaders — in promoting racial literacy.

---

[55] National Council of Teachers of English. (2019) "Definition of literacy in a digital age." https://ncte.org/statement/nctes-definition-literacy-digital-age

The teaching done by today's school librarians is much more dynamic and far-reaching than many realize. This dynamism and potential to make such a big impact in schools were largely what drew me to school librarianship in the first place. I'm very excited to share with you how we're teaching these multiple literacies and the positive impact that doing so has on our students.

In this chapter, I'll first define each of these literacies so we have a common language, and therefore a common understanding, of what I mean when I use these terms in the context of K-12 education. Then, I'll share why more educators need to teach these literacies across grade levels and subject areas, and detail some of the challenges you might face if you attempt to incorporate the teaching of any of these literacies into your practice. For each challenge, I'll include some advice for working through it.

Next, I'll walk you through some innovative examples of how today's school librarians are teaching these literacies to K-12 students — including examples from my own work and the work of other school librarians throughout the US. This will be followed by a few takeaways for all educators — teachers and administrators alike — who feel compelled to incorporate the teaching of some of these literacies into their own teaching practice or school leadership initiatives. Finally, I'll explain how you can tap your school librarians to help with this work.

Textual literacy

Let's start with the work that school librarians are best known for. Textual literacy is what most of us think of when we hear or see the word "literacy" — that is, the ability to read and write effectively.

Textual literacy refers to the understanding of how and why language works on the page and the many ways it can be used in one's own writing. Textual literacy involves meaning-making, interpretation, and analysis of the written word, all of which require not only reading comprehension but also critical thinking skills.

For many, the prevailing assumption about school librarians is that we only teach textual literacy and that, even within this literacy, we teach only one side of the coin: how to read, or how to read well. But school librarians have always been involved with teaching students how to communicate effectively through the written word, too. After all, reading and writing are two sides of the same coin.

Teachers who teach textual literacy effectively help students do what Dorothy Barnhouse and Vicki Vinton, in their book *What Readers Really Do*, call "noticing and naming."[56] When you ask students to notice and name what's going in their minds throughout the reading and writing processes — and then you notice and name your own professional observations about what they say — you give them a better understanding of how reading and writing work. This kind of modeling is at the heart of teaching textual literacy.

Visual literacy

Visual literacy is often overlooked and/or trivialized, yet you only need to think about how much we take for granted the ability to effectively and efficiently interpret visual information in books, films, TV, advertisements, and more to get a sense of how essential visual literacy really is to navigating life. A helpful definition of visual literacy comes from the Association of College and Research Libraries, a division of the American Library Association. Because it's written with higher education in mind, this definition can help K-12 educators understand exactly what is entailed in developing high-order visual literacy skills:

> *Visual literacy is a set of abilities that enables an individual to effectively find, interpret, evaluate, use, and create images and visual media. Visual literacy skills equip a learner to understand and analyze the contextual, cultural, ethical, aesthetic, intellectual, and technical components involved in the production and use of visual materials. A visually literate individual is both a critical consumer of visual media and a competent contributor to a body of shared knowledge and culture.*[57]

---

56   Barnhouse, D. & Vinton, V. (2012) *What Readers Really Do: Teaching the Process of Meaning Making*, Heinemann
57   Association of College and Research Libraries. (2011) "ACRL visual literacy competency standards for higher education," www.ala.org/acrl/standards/visualliteracy

Like textual literacy, visual literacy is twofold: there's the process of "reading" images (critically consuming them) and there's being proficient in creating them. If we only teach students how to critically consume images without giving them plentiful opportunities to practice creating their own effective imagery, we deprive them of the chance to develop a truly deep understanding of how images work.

Especially in the current era, where skewed information or outright lies abound in countless images circulated widely on the internet, visual literacy is essential. As Todd Finley writes in an article for *Edutopia*, "students need to respectfully question the author's authority, articulate what is represented and how, and infer what has been excluded and why."[58] When we teach visual literacy, we give students critical thinking skills that will help them in many parts of their lives.

Information literacy

Given the ways in which misinformation led to the insurrection at the US Capitol on January 6, 2021, information literacy has never been more important to teach. A helpful definition comes from the nonprofit organization Common Sense:

> *Information literacy includes the ability to identify, find, evaluate, and use information effectively. From effective search strategies to evaluation techniques, students learn how to evaluate the quality, credibility, and validity of websites, and give proper credit. Information literacy has also been referred to as digital literacy or media literacy. Regardless of the terminology, be it digital literacy or media literacy, having information literacy skills are the fundamentals to thrive in a digital space.*[59]

In this chapter, I differentiate between information literacy and digital literacy, the latter of which I'll define in the next section.

School librarians have always been leaders when it comes to teaching information literacy. And since the advent of the internet, most information is now found online, rather than in encyclopedias, books,

---

58   Finley, T. (2014) "Common Core in action: 10 visual literacy strategies,"
      www.edutopia.org/blog/ccia-10-visual-literacy-strategies-todd-finley
59   www.commonsense.org/education/digital-citizenship/information-literacy

and other print resources. But the essence of this work, for librarians and other educators, has remained the same: helping students learn what makes information reliable, how to read information with a critical eye, and how to confirm or deny the truthfulness or accuracy of information through other reliable sources.

Issues like political polarization have made it increasingly difficult to discern between fact and opinion online. Other problems compound this polarization, including self-created online echo chambers, in which we only interact with people and information that confirm our biases, and social media "filter bubbles," in which social media companies use algorithms that determine what kind of information we probably want to see and then show us only that information.[60] Being able to discern between fact and opinion is another crucial component of information literacy.

Finally, information literacy necessarily includes understanding how to create information. More specifically, understanding how to create information means understanding how to do so ethically (including properly citing sources), how to curate and synthesize a diversity of viewpoints, how to keep in mind one's audience, and even how to communicate one's own perspective in creative and engaging ways. These are all elements of information literacy that educators must teach explicitly.

Digital literacy

Although similar to information literacy, digital literacy often refers more specifically to the ability to successfully navigate various forms of online media. Some organizations and institutions consider digital literacy and information literacy to be synonymous. However, in my own usage — and for the purposes of this chapter — I differentiate between the two.

Common Sense provides a clear and helpful definition:

---

60   Pariser, E. (2011) "Beware online 'filter bubbles'" (video). TED, www.ted.com/talks/eli_pariser_beware_online_filter_bubbles

Digital literacy specifically applies to media from the internet, smartphones, video games, and other nontraditional sources. Just as media [or information] literacy includes the ability to identify media and its messages and create media responsibly, digital literacy includes both nuts-and-bolts skills and ethical obligations.[61]

Walking students through how to use a particular app that will be utilized in class is an example of teaching digital literacy. Given the amount of time young people spend online, teaching them how to use online media effectively and efficiently is very important. Digital literacy helps provide young people with the skills they need to be proficient online communicators.

Technological literacy

Given ongoing rapid advancements in technology and the extent to which technology will be used in the jobs that many of our students will seek, technological literacy is essential. Here's a great definition from the International Technology and Engineering Educators Association:

The term "technological literacy" refers to one's ability to use, manage, evaluate, and understand technology … In order to be a technologically literate citizen, a person should understand what technology is, how it works, how it shapes society and in turn how society shapes it. Moreover, a technologically literate person has some abilities to "do" technology that enables them to use their inventiveness to design and build things and to solve practical problems that are technological in nature. A characteristic of a technologically literate person is that they are comfortable with and objective about the use of technology, neither scared of it nor infatuated with it.[62]

Teaching young people how to "do" technology in a balanced way is a worthy goal. It's also a necessary one, because of the demands of the modern workplace. But we must maintain a critical mind about the ways in which we use technology with young people.

---

61 www.commonsensemedia.org/news-and-media-literacy/what-is-digital-literacy
62 www.iteea.org/48897.aspx

In terms of not becoming "infatuated" with technology, in my own work I try to keep in mind the perspective of Wendell Berry, the writer and poet — and one of my heroes. In a 2019 interview with Berry published by *The Christian Science Monitor*, interviewer Travis Kitchens writes:

> *Three decades after publishing his controversial 1988 essay "Why I Am Not Going to Buy a Computer" in* Harper's Magazine, *Mr. Berry still doesn't own one. He doesn't have a smartphone either.*
>
> *That perspective has lent the octogenarian a unique view of the role of technology in this increasingly digitized world. From behind his typewriter, he has remained skeptical about what he sees as "a technological fundamentalism," or blind faith in computers to liberate humanity.*[63]

It may seem somewhat strange to include Berry's radical stance when defining technological literacy. I'm certainly not advocating that we do not teach technological literacy — too much of the modern world requires a level of technological proficiency. What I'm trying to suggest is that we must develop and/or maintain a critical mind about how we use technology in K-12 education. We have to avoid "technological fundamentalism," in which technology is used for technology's sake or is pitched as something that will solve all humanity's problems.

Teaching students to be discerning about how and when they use technology is a critical part of technological literacy. In K-12 education, we must be intentional about how we use technology and avoid the trap of using it just because we can or think we should. This way, we can focus on equipping our students with foundational technology skills — including a healthy mindset about technology's possibilities and limitations — that they can build upon as technologies change and evolve.

Racial literacy

In the summer of 2020, the US experienced what has been called a racial reckoning, sparked by the murder of George Floyd, an unarmed 46-year-old Black man, by a Minneapolis police officer on May 25,

---

63   Kitchens, T. (2019) "Why Wendell Berry is still not going to buy a computer," *The Christian Science Monitor.* www.csmonitor.com/Technology/2019/0418/Why-Wendell-Berry-is-still-not-going-to-buy-a-computer

2020 — recorded on a smartphone and shared for all the world to see. Our country has a long history of violence and oppression toward Black, Indigenous, and people of color (BIPOC), and Floyd's murder led many people to consider the systemic nature of racism. And many started to become more vocal and active in addressing this systemic racism.

As K-12 educators, we are charged with preparing young people for the world they will inherit. Therefore, we have no choice but to address race, racism, white supremacy, and the importance of anti-racism. One of the essential ways we do this is by teaching racial literacy.

I'm going to share two different definitions of racial literacy. They both address different aspects of what it means to be racially literate, and I think they're both helpful and important. The first comes from the author and professor Dr. Howard C. Stevenson. In his book *Promoting Racial Literacy in Schools*, Stevenson defines racial literacy as "the ability to read, recast, and resolve racially stressful social interactions."[64]

Stevenson notes that reading racially stressful social interactions means successfully interpreting what is happening. Recasting means noticing what's happening in one's body and using stress-reducing strategies. Resolving means striving to respond justly while not overreacting.[65]

In a short lecture recorded at the University of Pennsylvania, where Stevenson is the Constance Clayton professor of urban education and professor of Africana studies, he discusses the importance of teachers developing their own racial literacy for the benefit of their students. This way, when difficult moments around race come up in schools, teachers are equipped to respond in positive ways. Of teachers, Stevenson says, "We would love ... [them] to know themselves in those moments and make decisions without overreacting and particularly without using force or violence as a way to resolve this sense of threat that many of us feel when we don't want to be embarrassed or don't want to look like we're incompetent. Our young people need it."[66]

---

64   Stevenson, H.C. (2014) *Promoting Racial Literacy in Schools: Differences That Make a Difference*, Teachers College Press

65   The Brainwaves Video Anthology. "Howard Stevenson — promoting racial literacy in schools" (video), YouTube. https://youtu.be/fzuS7oK7Ux8

66   Ibid.

Perhaps it goes without saying that in order to teach literacy, you must be literate yourself. For none of the literacies discussed in this chapter is this more pivotal than racial literacy. If we're racially literate in the sense that Stevenson describes then we can help give students the tools they need to navigate our racialized world — and, with ongoing effort, to be anti-racist themselves.

The second definition of racial literacy that we'll consider for this chapter comes from Lani Guinier, a professor at Harvard Law School. In her highly influential article "From racial liberalism to racial literacy," Guinier writes that racial literacy requires us to consider the ways in which race "invariably shapes educational, economic, and political opportunities for all of us."[67] I find this definition helpful to consider alongside Stevenson's, as it forces us to keep in mind the importance of knowing about — and talking about — the implications of living in a racialized world.

In other words, being racially literate means not only being comfortable talking about race, but also knowing *how* to talk about race.

Overcoming challenges

The multiple literacies we're exploring in this chapter are necessary to teach across grade levels and subject areas. This isn't to say that we all need to teach these literacies all the time; rather, we must identify how and where we could work them into our teaching and school leadership. After all, these are literacies that all students need in order to fully participate in society and to fully contribute to society.

In your own efforts to integrate these literacies into your practice, you will face challenges on the front end. And you'll face challenges as you develop your approach to teaching them.

Time

For most educators, the biggest impediment to doing anything new or different is time. Perhaps you've said it yourself on countless occasions, as I have: "I'd love to _____, if I just had the time." But these multiple literacies

---

67   Guinier, L. (2004) "From racial liberalism to racial literacy: Brown v. Board of Education and the interest-divergence dilemma," *Journal of American History*, 91(1), 92–118

are so important that we must figure out ways to promote them in our schools. Put simply, these literacies are essential for young people coming of age in the 21st century. If you teach, I would urge you to do whatever you can to make time, even just a little, to look at your curricula through the lens of each of these literacies. You'll notice at least some opportunities to further promote them in your classroom. Several of these literacies are clearly interrelated, and several might also be interrelated to content in your curricula. It won't take a ton of time to figure out ways to further promote them in units and lessons that already exist.

Questions of relevance

Maybe you or those you work with are concerned that these literacies aren't directly related to the subject or perhaps even the grade level that you teach. This is a fair concern. But aren't there certain skills that most of us already agree need to be taught across grade levels and subject areas, such as critical thinking skills? This question points to what some have called the "metacurriculum." In *Interdisciplinary Curriculum*, David Ackerman and D.N. Perkins define the metacurriculum as being "comprised of learning skills and strategies selected on the basis of their value in helping students (1) acquire the curriculum content being taught and (2) develop the capacity to think and learn independently."[68] Plenty of educators have advocated for textual literacy as part of the metacurriculum. But there has yet to be a big enough push for promoting visual, digital, technological, and racial literacies across grade levels and subject areas.

After just a little thoughtful planning, teaching these literacies more directly in all classrooms can help us deepen students' understanding of almost any subject or topic. For example, if students are researching specific states for their third-grade social studies class, it's enormously helpful for them to have a few lessons on exactly how to find and evaluate information. And perhaps these same students are then tasked with creating some kind of online, visual synthesis of the reliable information they found about their state — digital trading cards, for example, or

---

68   Ackerman, D. & Perkins, D.N. (1989) "Integrating thinking and learning skills across the curriculum," in Hayes Jacobs, H. (ed) *Interdisciplinary Curriculum: Design and Implementation*, ACSD

perhaps even a website. It would certainly be worth including mini-lessons on apps they could use (digital literacy), as well as mini-lessons on choosing colors, choosing fonts, and/or perhaps even the rule of thirds (visual literacy). Teaching these literacies more explicitly and more often can help educators cover their content more deeply. If we begin to think about these multiple literacies as part of the metacurriculum — skills that help all students in all contexts — then the question of relevance quickly begins to disappear.

Lack of understanding or experience

In order to successfully teach any of these literacies, educators must first have a certain level of understanding of what exactly these literacies are, how to effectively teach them, and why they should be taught as part of the metacurriculum. Administrators can create ongoing learning opportunities for faculty during regularly scheduled faculty meetings and any in-house professional development sessions. In most schools, there's plenty of in-house expertise that can be tapped to lead these learning opportunities. I also encourage all educators to either create or engage with some kind of professional learning network (PLN). Email lists (also known as listservs), Facebook groups, and Twitter chats provide online opportunities for engaging with other educators about these literacies and, really, any topic of interest to educators. As someone who actively participates in various PLNs, I cannot stress enough the extent to which they can help you learn and grow.

Visiting other schools is an incredibly helpful way to learn more about how these literacies can be taught. You just need to find a school — perhaps through your PLN — that models successful promotion of these literacies, and then schedule a visit to observe and ideally chat with a few teachers or administrators. At the very least you'll come away with new ideas about how to approach this work in your classroom, department, or whole school. Any progress you can make individually or collectively within your school toward students becoming "multiliterate"[69] is worthwhile.

---

69   Arnone, M.P. & Reynolds, R. (2009) "Empirical support for the integration of dispositions in action and multiple literacies into AASL's Standards for the 21st Century Learner," American Association of School Librarians. https://files.eric. ed.gov/fulltext/EJ877494.pdf

School libraries leading the way

School librarians are made for this work. Here are two crucial points from a 2009 presentation shared by an AASL (American Association of School Librarians) task force:

- "School library media specialists [librarians] have the expertise in multiple literacies to collaborate with teachers for effective teaching and learning."
- "[School librarians] can make a positive impact on students' engagement with texts and reading development by working with other educators to integrate multiple literacies into the classroom curriculum. These literacies are critical learning objectives for 21st century learners."[70]

My own work in promoting multiple literacies begins with my second graders. In Chapter 3, I described how, in lieu of a traditional library story time, I design various learning stations each week for second-grade students to explore when they come into the library. As you can probably imagine, creating multiple learning stations is a perfect way to teach multiple literacies. I can target one or more literacies at any given station, and I can make adjustments week to week according to students' needs. Below are a few examples of learning stations I've created for my second graders. For each, I state which of the multiple literacies I'm aiming to teach or promote.

- **Finding fun facts.** I create and lay out a small, themed collection of nonfiction picture books, often related to a topic the students are studying in language arts, social studies, or science. In a form included at this station, students identify one fun fact they learned while skimming one of the books, and they also cite their source by recording the author's name and the title of the book. This is my introductory approach to teaching citation, an important element of information literacy.

---

70   SLMS Role in Reading Task Force. (2009) "What every SLMS should know about teaching multiple literacy strategies" (presentation), American Association of School Librarians. www.ala.org/aasl/files/aaslissues/toolkits/slroleinreading/rrtfmultipleliteracies.ppt

- **Recommendation bookmarks.** At this station, I lay out printed bookmarks that say "_____ recommends this book because..." at the very top. Students must first think of a library book they borrowed, finished, and enjoyed recently, perhaps one they read in the past week. Next, they write their name in the blank space and explain one very specific reason they would recommend the book to other students — for example, "The main character made me laugh again and again." Then they locate the book in the library and insert their recommendation bookmark so the top is visible. This has been a wonderful way to promote textual literacy, because when students see these bookmarks throughout the library they're more likely to give the books a try. The students who recommend these books also practice their writing skills. They're not doing *much* writing, obviously, but these one-sentence reviews are a great way to teach them how to evaluate a text with specificity.

- **E-book collections.** Before class, I connect with the classroom teachers to learn what topics are being covered at that time, and I curate a small collection of related (directly or tangentially) e-books using Epic, a student-friendly digital library. Then I make sure there are four iPads — we have a cart of them in our library — with the Epic app loaded and ready to go. Some books on Epic also have audio or video components, so I make sure headphones are available. The nonfiction books I curate for this station are short and accessible, and students only need to read one before moving on to another station. This has been a really helpful way to further familiarize students with the iPads (technological literacy), which are still fairly new to some students, while also familiarizing them with e-reading apps like Epic (digital literacy). Not to mention the time spent reading (textual literacy)!

- **Pattern play.** This station is centered around a puzzle created by the company MindWare. Students work individually or in small groups (three students is a good maximum) to piece together the puzzle, which consists of 40 wooden blocks in various colors. It comes with 40 pattern cards that students must work to reproduce using the pieces of the puzzle. They choose a single pattern card to focus on for their time at this station. This has been a great way to teach visual literacy, specifically how to use color and shapes and how to create symmetry. Students have a real sense of accomplishment after they finish creating their selected pattern.

Any time I introduce a new station, I give students a quick run-through of how it works at the beginning of class. Whenever I feel it's necessary, I include printed directions at particular stations so students can see and reference the steps they need to follow. It takes time to set all this up, of course. But once the stations are set up, the class pretty much runs itself. I'm able to move from station to station myself, offer help when needed, and manage the flow. This model works well across grade levels and subject areas, because its structure — multiple stations — is naturally conducive to teaching multiple literacies.

I take a different approach to teaching multiple literacies with the other elementary grades. Several years ago I worked directly with our technology integrationist to develop a new class that we co-plan and co-teach each week in the third and fourth grades. For this class, my goal is to teach 21st century library skills, and the technology integrationist's goal is to teach digital and technological skills. Given the overlap in our roles — digital literacy and technological literacy are in my purview, too — we decided it would be beneficial to teach students together in a new, experimental hybrid class.

This didn't happen overnight, of course. We spent a lot of time envisioning what this class should look like and working with administrators to make it happen in the schedule. To be clear, this is my weekly library class with both these grades; I don't have a separate teaching block with these students. I was able to work with the classroom teachers to move student book browsing and checkout to different scheduled times each week so that I could maximize our teaching and learning time. This has proven enormously helpful. Of course, we consulted the classroom teachers on the lesson content. In fact, we often co-plan and co-teach with them, and we typically teach inside the third and fourth-grade classrooms.

The idea behind this class is that we do some kind of project-based deep dive into a topic students are *already studying* elsewhere in their grade-level curriculum — usually in science, language arts, or social studies. We call this weekly class "library and technology integration," and we're honestly a bit hesitant to call it a "class" because it's not meant to exist as a standalone curriculum. We want to help students learn library- and technology-specific skills through ongoing, integrated learning opportunities that directly connect with what they're learning elsewhere in their curriculum, rather than facilitating unrelated, one-off lessons on our own each week. Sometimes we break the class into two groups — I'll take one half and the technology integrationist will take the other — to teach specific skills in a targeted way. But we always start together and we usually end together.

One project example from our weekly library and technology integration with the third grade is centered around the study of animals and their habitats. This project began with students studying specific animals in language arts class. The technology integrationist, the third-grade teachers, and I decided it would be helpful and fun to have students do some kind of related project with us, in which students did more in-depth research about their animal and their animal's habitat. We wanted the project to culminate with each student creating some kind of visual depicting their chosen animal in its habitat, with each element of the habitat supported by the information they researched.

We've repeated this project several times now and it has been a wonderful way to teach multiple literacies. The third-grade teachers and I focus on textual literacy by connecting students with books about their chosen animals. I teach information literacy through mini-lessons on using keywords to search elementary-level databases, navigating the databases themselves, and paraphrasing and citing the information that students find. The technology integrationist and I teach technological literacy by helping students with the basics of using their laptops, which are new to them in third grade, and digital and visual literacy through CoSpaces, a coding and augmented reality app. The technology integrationist takes the lead on teaching the elementary-level coding that allows students to depict their chosen animal moving about their virtual habitat. And I take the lead on ensuring that the information depicted visually in the virtual habitat is properly cited and, well, accurate.

Toward the end of the project, we work together to further promote digital and visual literacy by helping students fully utilize the digital tools within CoSpaces to create an interactive animal habitat — animal included, of course — that is visually appealing to their audience. The interactive habitat must be neatly organized and colorful, and the imagery included must be easily understood or interpreted. When we share links to these projects with parents and other faculty members, they're always impressed. The digital technology is definitely cool, but most importantly it's used in a meaningful way that involves genuine inquiry and creative expression.

Not all the projects we facilitate during this library and technology integration time promote multiple literacies to the same extent, but many of them do. The project-based nature of this class, combined with the fact that multiple teachers with multiple skillsets are involved each week, allows multiple literacies to be easily taught in context.

My technology integrationist colleague and I run the same kind of course with our fifth graders, with the notable difference that instead of facilitating multiple projects throughout the year, students work on one project for the entire school year. We call this the Passion Project (I outline the basics of how we facilitate it in Chapter 1). This works exceptionally well in helping us teach multiple literacies to students.

All in all, I cannot recommend this collaborative, project-based teaching approach enough to anyone interested in promoting multiple literacies. It's such a dynamic way to teach students the specific skills they need to navigate our complex, interconnected world. Not only that, but for me it's so gratifying seeing or hearing a teacher pointing students to a resource I identified or taught previously. This is a fantastic byproduct of this kind of co-teaching and collaboration. There are ripple effects throughout the school.

I also work with middle school students, although I don't have scheduled classes with them each week. They come to our student-staffed writing center, which lives in one of the small study rooms in the back of our library. This writing center, discussed in Chapter 2, is staffed by a group of about 10 eighth-grade student mentors that I train to work with their peers. It's a powerful way to promote textual literacy beyond just helping students learn to read well. Students are encouraged to visit the center during any stage of the writing process (brainstorming, drafting, revision, or editing) for any writing in any class.

The writing center has allowed our library to become a place where students learn to write well. This has been enormously helpful in expanding my school's perception of the library. Faculty, students, and parents alike have come to see that the library is more than just a place where information is consumed; it's also a place where information is *created*. In my mind, this is one of the crucial attributes of the 21st century school library.

In terms of promoting and teaching racial literacy, I want to first point out that I see my own racial literacy as a never-ending work in progress. This is definitely the case for me with the other literacies, as well, but I've learned that it's especially important to keep this in mind when it comes to racial literacy, or else I risk becoming ignorant and/or causing students harm. Remaining open to learning, especially from BIPOC writers and educators, is critical. As such, I try to cultivate a growth mindset toward racial literacy.

In a conversation with *School Library Journal*, Kathy Carroll, the 2020-21 president of the American Association of School Libraries (AASL), discussed the role that school librarians play in teaching racial literacy — particularly the destructive role and impact of white supremacy:

> *School librarians must face these subjects in a facts-first, age-appropriate way that doesn't suggest the educator is uncomfortable in any way or afraid to discuss it, [Carroll] says. Students can sniff out that fear.*

> *"If you lose credibility with them personally, you're going to lose it with them when you're trying to have an academic conversation," says Carroll, library media specialist at Westwood High School in Columbia, SC. "It's all about relationships."*[71]

---

71   Yorio, K. (2021) "Librarians uniquely equipped to address the tenor of the times," *School Library Journal*. www.slj.com/librarians-uniquely-equipped-to-address-tenor-of-the-times-covid-19-coronavirus-school-librarians

As a reminder, I operate from two definitions of racial literacy — one of which comes from Howard C. Stevenson, who says that it's "the ability to read, recast, and resolve racially stressful social interactions."[72] For many teachers, including myself on many occasions, simply talking about race can be stressful. In my own work toward becoming more racially literate, I make sure reading and talking about race is something that's regularly part of my professional development. Having ongoing opportunities to read, think, and talk about race — such as through the National SEED (Seeking Educational Equity and Diversity) Project, which I highly recommend — really has made me better equipped to read, recast, and do my best to resolve racially stressful moments when they arise in the classroom.

Because of the nature of the library classes I teach, I don't facilitate traditional literary discussions about books nearly as often as I did when I was an English teacher. This doesn't mean I no longer have opportunities to teach the kind of racial literacy that Lani Guinier describes, which involves helping students understand the ways in which race "invariably shapes educational, economic, and political opportunities for all of us."[73] This teaching happens occasionally when I'm helping students consider the impact of race on topics they're researching, for example. But, mostly, in my role as school librarian I promote racial literacy through the books I buy, display, and recommend to students.

There's this lingering, troublesome theory out there that White kids are not interested in books featuring BIPOC protagonists. In my experience, this is completely untrue. Take, for example, the "Surprise Me!" book recommendation program I started recently — an idea I borrowed from Kelsey Bogan, whom you'll hear from in the next section. This program consists of sharing with students a very straightforward Google Form in which they use checkboxes and answer questions about what kind of books they like. Then we (me and/or my library assistant) pick out new books for them.

---

72   Stevenson, H.C. (2014) *Promoting Racial Literacy in Schools: Differences That Make a Difference*, Teachers College Press

73   Guinier, L. (2004) "From racial liberalism to racial literacy: Brown v. Board of Education and the interest-divergence dilemma," *Journal of American History*, 91(1), 92–118

This has proven to be an excellent way to introduce students to books that center BIPOC voices. If the story is engaging — if it's a good book — then students enjoy it. And in the process they learn about identities and experiences that are different from their own. This is the great power of fiction.

To this point, Ijeoma Oluo, author of *So You Want To Talk About Race*,[74] has shared some related wisdom with *School Library Journal*:

> *We talk about the beauty of imagination and books, right? You can imagine yourself being anything. But that sentiment usually comes from people who always see some sort of representation of themselves in the books. But if [people in books] never look like you, that sends a message too. That actually activates your imagination in a negative way—that you never see a black scientist, you never see an Asian politician. These things limit. The amount of imagination we're asking of our young people of color is astounding.*
>
> *But it also affects white students, because it limits what they think their classmates of color can do. This has a real impact on how we see the world, how we support our systems. The young people are the carriers of our systems. They're going to inherit it all, and we need them to imagine something better, something more inclusive. We nurture that by showing diverse voices, showing diverse histories, and really giving them a new idea.*[75]

Indeed, each "new idea" goes a long way toward promoting and teaching racial literacy. The more opportunities we give students to read what the organization We Need Diverse Books calls "literature that reflects and honors the lives of all young people,"[76] the better.

Forward-thinking librarians

Kelsey Bogan, school librarian at Great Valley High School in Malvern, Pennsylvania, loves teaching multiple literacies. In my conversation with

74   Oluo, I. (2018) *So You Want To Talk About Race*, Seal Press
75   Yorio, K. (2018) "Educators and race: a conversation with author Ijeoma Oluo on tackling systemic racism in U.S. education," *School Library Journal*. www.slj.com/educators-and-race-a-conversation-with-author-ijeoma-oluo-on-tackling-systemic-racism-in-us-education
76   https://diversebooks.org/about-wndb

her, she tells me about a mini-project she facilitates with 12th-grade English language arts students around Margaret Atwood's *The Handmaid's Tale.*

"We teach the students about the concept of modern propaganda strategy by learning about how color, symbol, and design theory combined with psychological manipulation techniques are used to create strong and manipulative visual messages," Bogan says. "Students apply these visual media literacies by analyzing modern political propaganda such as memes, social media posts, ads, and commercials. The culmination of the mini-unit tasks students with taking the role of a Gilead (the oppressive regime in the book) official and designing a social media graphic that acts as Gilead propaganda. They have to decide what tone and message they want to convey and then carefully select the color, font type and size, at least one symbol, and a line from the text that combine together to convey their chosen tone and message."

It's the kind of project that keeps students engaged and thinking critically, and it also serves as a great way to teach multiple literacies. "Each year I am amazed at how nuanced and impactful the graphics our students design are," Bogan says. "I love this mini-unit because it combines visual, information, technological, media, and even textual literacies."

Another project that Bogan loves for teaching multiple literacies is a collaboration with a pop culture elective. "I do a media literacy unit with them, teaching about how to learn to view and consume information with healthy skepticism and how to establish habits of 'quick checking' and 'quick evaluating' the sources of said information," Bogan says. She emphasizes that students must learn to be critical thinkers about all information they come across online. "This includes videos, social media posts, TikToks, memes, and advertisements," she notes, each of which students may not have felt the need to evaluate prior to this unit.

"The mini-unit culminates in students creating a meme that could be used to help bring awareness of the importance of evaluating information before believing it," Bogan adds. "This meme creation helps reinforce the learning but also helps reinforce the fact that it's easy and free for anyone to create and share content meant to convey a certain message. Plus, I think everyone has had enough of creating PowerPoint presentations — creating a simple meme instead is fun!" It's another unit that combines multiple literacies, with Bogan noting that through it she is able to teach visual, digital, technological, and information literacy.

Bogan also shares with me the importance of promoting multiple literacies "where colleagues can see." She notes that some teachers may not be comfortable teaching certain literacies, which is fair because many are expected to be specialists, not generalists like librarians. They also might not know they can turn to librarians for help with teaching these literacies. "This is why I talk about this stuff so frequently in my newsletters, staff meeting remarks, social media posts, and professional development workshops for faculty," she says. "This helps make my colleagues aware that this is something I can and will help them bring to their students. It's primarily an advocacy issue, because so many of our colleagues still associate the role of the librarian specifically — and sometimes solely — with books, and therefore they don't immediately think to collaborate with us on multiple literacy needs. Once they know it's something we *can* do, and that helping them is something we *want* to do, it's much easier to secure those collaborative opportunities."

Andrea Trudeau, school librarian at Alan B. Shepard Middle School in Deerfield, Illinois, is another huge advocate of teaching multiple literacies. For her, it's all about integrating them as much as possible into what we teach our students every day — or, as we called it earlier in the chapter, the metacurriculum. "Rather than setting aside a designated block of time or creating standalone lessons taught out of context to promote a particular literacy, it's vital to weave multiple literacies into the critical work we do each and every day with students," she tells me. Trudeau argues that this integrated approach can only happen through a concerted effort by educators throughout each school building, and when librarians play a leading role.

As the recipient of the 2020 AASL Frances Henne Award — which honors a school librarian "who demonstrates leadership qualities with students, teachers, and administrators" — Trudeau is clearly passionate about leadership. For her, leadership is largely about collaboration and integration. "I partner with teachers in the lessons, assignments, and projects they design and implement with students," she says. "These partnerships have become a powerful vehicle for me in regards to teaching multiple literacies, since they allow me to not only incorporate skills into the lessons that I deliver, but they also provide me with opportunities for impactful behind-the-scenes conversations with colleagues about the importance of multiple literacies and how best to reinforce them."

Trudeau tells me about a seventh-grade social studies project in which she collaborated with both teachers and students. This project involved students exploring different countries throughout the world, and Trudeau met with teachers before the unit began. "I work diligently to stay abreast of current digital and technological tools and determine which are most effective in supporting pedagogy," she says. "In this case, I worked with the social studies teachers to ensure they had a general understanding of each application that students would use to demonstrate their learning — including Powtoon, WeVideo, and CoSpaces Edu." Trudeau helped teachers develop this "menu" of digital options, and she went on to create tutorial screencasts and other resources for students. She also taught mini-lessons related to each of the apps, and provided individualized feedback and troubleshooting assistance. Through this kind of collaborative, integrated approach to teaching, Trudeau was able to teach visual, digital, and technological literacies to students and teachers.

"For one teacher, the plan for teaching multiple literacies may mean I take the lead and teach the lesson to model it for the teacher," Trudeau says. "For another teacher, it may mean the teacher and I co-teach the lesson together. And for yet another, it may mean I meet with the teacher to devise a plan where the teacher ultimately teaches or leads the lesson. Just as we differentiate instruction for our students, I differentiate support and instruction for my colleagues with the ultimate goal in mind of promoting multiple literacies for our students."

Takeaways for all educators

Perhaps the most important takeaway regarding multiple literacies is approaching them as part of the metacurriculum. If we can all agree that each of the literacies discussed in this chapter is crucial to our students' success in the 21st century, then we can begin promoting and teaching them with greater urgency.

If you're a teacher compelled to teach multiple literacies, regardless of your subject matter or grade level, then I suggest you begin by considering your strengths. Once you determine which of the literacies you feel most comfortable and competent teaching, you can consider how you could double down and teach them more explicitly — or in greater depth. A quick look at upcoming unit or lesson plans through this lens will surely spark some ideas. Then you can begin considering which of the literacies you don't teach as effectively or perhaps at all.

To become more literate yourself, you'll likely find at least some helpful information online. Personally, I find that I have more luck with buying or borrowing educational books related to the topic I'm exploring. I don't always read them in their entirety, but educational books often have more details and examples than you can find through searching Google. There are numerous great books about each of the literacies we have discussed in this chapter. You can search for them yourself or ask your school librarian for specific recommendations.

Another option is hopping on a social networking site like Twitter or Facebook and connecting with educators who might be able to share their ideas or experiences. There are various Twitter chats you can participate in, and there are many educator groups you can join on Facebook. You can search within these networks for what other educators have said about the literacy or literacies you're researching, and you can also pose specific questions yourself. I'm always surprised by the breadth of ideas that other educators share whenever I inquire about something related to my own work as a librarian.

You might also consider observing another educator, either in your school or elsewhere, whom you know has some experience — perhaps even expertise — in teaching the literacy or literacies you're interested in. Or perhaps you'd like to dive right in and co-teach a lesson or unit with them. You can both teach to your specialty or specialties, and as your colleague teaches their students you'll have the benefit of learning alongside them.

Finally, you can always seek out professional development opportunities — classes, workshops, conferences, etc. — that seem relevant and likely to increase your own understanding of the literacies you're studying. With workshops and conferences, you can seek out individual sessions that cover the specific literacies you're looking to learn more about. It can be tough to find the right opportunity at the right time, but when you do the face time with other committed educators it is almost always worth the effort. There are lots of great options out there for not only teaching specific literacies but also teaching multiple literacies at once, especially through project-based learning, inquiry-based learning, and design thinking, each of which I outline in Chapter 1.

Whichever route(s) you take to increase your own knowledge about multiple literacies, you'll surely find new and innovative ways to bring them into the metacurriculum at your school. I find that taking a more multimodal approach to my own lessons and units invariably makes teaching and learning more interesting, more rigorous, and more fun.

Administrators, if you'd like to better incorporate these multiple literacies into the metacurriculum at your school, then I suggest first identifying where specific literacies are taught in your school curricula. You can lead this work yourself or assign it to an educator who oversees curricula. If neither of those are possible then you could start a committee tasked with identifying where these literacies are being taught. Whoever leads the work, the essence of it should be talking with teachers about where these literacies are being taught — which subjects, grades, etc. — and where they are not. Just be sure to stress to faculty that this is purely observational (as opposed to evaluative) and that you're looking for ways to better integrate these literacies throughout the school. I would also recommend defining the metacurriculum and being clear that this is about making these literacies part of it.

Once you've gathered this information, you can plan and/or design professional development opportunities within your school that will help faculty gain essential understandings of — and confidence in — each of the literacies. Or you can research and compile a list of related learning opportunities outside your school that faculty could attend, and then do your best to pitch and fund these opportunities. Additionally, the person(s) leading this work can begin working with teachers to support them in their ongoing efforts to learn and teach multiple literacies.

How your librarian can help

Teachers, your school librarian is well versed in promoting and teaching multiple literacies and we can help you in various ways. Below are just a few approaches you could take in making use of us as in-house resources.

- **Curating resources.** If you're crunched for time or would just like someone with research expertise to help you gather some resources about specific literacies, let your librarian know. We can curate resources for you that will give you an overview of the literacies you're curious about teaching, or go in-depth into one or more of them — whichever suits your experience and/ or interest level. Speaking from experience, this is the kind of service that teachers don't often think they can turn to their school librarian for, but we're more than happy to help. We're well connected and can put together a customized collection of resources for you relatively quickly. Either independently or in conjunction with our technology-focused colleagues, we can also provide you with curated lists of digital apps and other tools that can help you teach these literacy skills to your students. Think of this as just another service offered by your school library.

- **Leading workshops.** You're always welcome to ask your school librarian to lead a workshop or series of workshops on any of the literacies you'd like to better understand. We can share our own experience with teaching multiple literacies and accordingly can recommend specific multimodal approaches, tools, resources, and more. Keep in mind that these workshops don't have to be big, formal events within the school; we can sit down with small groups of teachers and walk you through our recommendations. We're flexible. Whatever the format, whatever the structure, it's part of our job to actively promote and teach these literacies — and we'll do what we can to make sure they're being taught consistently throughout our schools.

- **Co-planning and/or co-teaching.** We're happy to sit down with you, look at and/or discuss your curriculum, and help you figure out concrete ways to integrate multiple literacies into your teaching. This kind of co-planning works really well for some teachers, and librarians love this kind of collaboration. Just tell us on the front end which of the literacies you're looking to teach — or teach with more precision — and we'll help you consider your plans through that lens. Along the way we'll offer specific suggestions, and there's a good chance these conversations could lead to teaching collaborations for lessons, projects, or even whole units.

Administrators, if you're feeling compelled to integrate these literacies into curricula throughout your school, talk to your school librarian. We can help you brainstorm ways to make this happen. In *BiblioTech*, John Palfrey shares why:

> *Teachers are rarely well trained in coming up with new materials or teaching new media and technology. Some are extremely savvy technology users, but most teachers were students before digital technologies became as central to the learning process as they are today. School librarians are trained in exactly these processes, both in graduate school as they earn master's degrees in library and information sciences and on the job in internships or first jobs out of school.*[77]

You should also know that we're committed to this work because we really do believe these literacies are crucial for navigating life in the 21st century. The AASL Standards Framework notes that today's school librarians strive to make sure "learners [are] prepared for college, career, and life."[78] As such, we feel strongly that textual, visual, information, digital, technological, and racial literacies should be actively promoted and taught in our schools. We're happy to help you lead the charge. We can share resources, teach faculty, and launch new initiatives that will help you ensure that each of these literacies are part of your school's metacurriculum.

---

77 Palfrey, J. (2015) *BiblioTech: Why Libraries Matter More Than Ever in the Age of Google*, Basic Books

78 American Association of School Librarians. (2018) *AASL Standards Framework for Learners*, American Library Association. https://standards.aasl.org/wp-content/uploads/2017/11/AASL-Standards-Framework-for-Learners-pamphlet.pdf

A truly literate person

In *Leading from the Library*, Shannon McClintock Miller and William Bass offer the following wisdom about the connection between multiple literacies and what it means for a person to be "literate" in the 21st century:

> *While it's convenient to label different topics as their own literacy, we feel that, when all is said and done, all of these topics come together and define what it means to be literate in today's world. Can one be "literate" in the digital age without having an understanding of the message of media or how to critically consume information? We would argue that they cannot, and the same holds true for many, if not all, of the "literacies" that we continue to define and subcategorize. We are not condemning these different labels. We recognize that sometimes it can help [to] define and explain a concept and give some common language. In this instance, we are just suggesting that all these "literacies" overlap and inform each other to create a truly literate person.*[79]

Below are some guiding questions that can help teachers and administrators begin to think critically about making sure each of our students is on track to become "a truly literate person."

Teachers:

- Which literacies are already part of your metacurriculum? Which literacies are you not teaching at all right now?
- Where and how could you learn more about the literacies that you aren't already teaching?
- How would making your teaching increasingly multimodal benefit your students?
- How might collaborating with your school librarian and/ or other colleagues make teaching multiple literacies more effective and enjoyable for you and your students?

---

79   McClintock Miller, S. & Bass, W. (2019) *Leading from the Library: Help Your School Community Thrive in the Digital Age*, International Society for Technology in Education

Administrators:
- How could you take an inventory of the multiple literacies currently being taught in your school? How could your school librarian help with this process?
- In your school, who are the experts in each of the literacies discussed in this chapter? How could they share their expertise with the rest of the faculty?
- What's the best way to communicate to faculty that these literacies are essential parts of the metacurriculum?
- How might a greater emphasis on multimodal teaching and learning better equip your students for the future?

Chapter 5

Building meaningful connections to the outside world

"Good teachers possess a capacity for connectedness. They are able to weave a complex web of connections among themselves, their subjects, and their students so that students can learn to weave a world for themselves"

— Parker J. Palmer

One of my favorite parts of working as a school librarian is connecting with so many different people throughout each day. From the parent volunteers who help us with shelving books to the many students and teachers who meet, learn, and create in the library, my days are filled with moments of connection. These in-person connections are incredibly valuable to me, especially in the wake of Covid-19.

The pandemic also highlighted, in extraordinary fashion, the ways in which we are all connected. The choices each of us make individually have an impact that goes beyond ourselves. Add to this the fact that we live in a digital age and it feels vital that we honor this great interconnectedness with our students. Schools can feel like insular places, which can be stifling and restrictive, especially for our students. But the moment we connect ourselves and our students with the world outside, teaching and learning become much more dynamic.

For students, building connections to the outside world makes the learning process more authentic — they know that what they're learning isn't disconnected from reality. For educators, building connections to the outside world energizes us, broadens our perspectives, and helps us develop new ideas.

This chapter explores specific ways in which school librarians actively work to build connections to the outside world for students. We'll look at how 21st century school librarians are cultivating digital citizenship and connecting students to the global learning community. I hope to give you a greater understanding of how 21st century school libraries help their constituents transcend the walls of the school — and how you can do this, too.

To begin, I'll share some essential elements of what it means for students to be good digital citizens, as well as what I mean by participating in the global learning community. These terms — "digital citizenship" and "global learning community" — are tossed around quite a bit in educational circles, and I want to make sure you know exactly what I mean when I use them throughout this chapter.

As in previous chapters, I'll also walk you through some challenges you might encounter as you work to build your own connections as an educator and build connections for your students. For each challenge, I'll include some advice for working through it. Next, I'll share some specific examples of how school librarians are leading this work, as well as some takeaways for educators of all stripes.

To conclude, I'll offer some suggestions for how you can better use your school librarian and school library to help you build the kinds of connections outlined in this chapter, culminating in a few guiding questions to get you thinking about either beginning this work or placing greater emphasis on it.

Digital citizenship

A clear and concise definition of digital citizenship comes from the Common Sense organization, which worked with Project Zero at Harvard University to develop a widely used curriculum for K-12 students: "Digital citizenship is the responsible use of technology to learn, create, and participate."[80]

Common Sense's digital citizenship curriculum is high-quality and used in many K-12 schools, so I'll briefly discuss its six central topics here. A quick overview of these topics will give us more specifics to discuss throughout the chapter. Below are my short summaries of the topics as they're framed in *Teaching Digital Citizens in Today's World*, a research-based report published by Common Sense.[81]

- **Media balance and wellbeing.** Our students spend much of their days online. It's important for them to learn how to find a sense of balance with their screen use, in terms of how much time they spend on their devices relative to other activities (such as reading or playing outside) and in terms of what activities they are doing on their devices. This self-reflection should be ongoing, always with an eye toward mental health and overall wellbeing.

- **Privacy and security.** Students need to be knowledgeable about their digital footprints and how to protect their privacy as much as possible. They must understand the risks involved in sharing information with others online, in addition to learning how doing so safely and responsibly can help them create positive connections.

- **Digital footprint and identity.** Using digital media can be an incredibly powerful way to express oneself and gain a better understanding of one's identity. For teens especially, digital media can also restrict this process by seemingly imposing certain norms about how to behave with others online. There's

---

80   James, C., Weinstein, E. & Mendoza, K. (2021) *Teaching Digital Citizens in Today's World: Research and Insights Behind the Common Sense K-12 Digital Citizenship Curriculum*, Common Sense
81   Ibid.

a pressure for many young people to look and speak in specific ways, which can be limiting and exhausting. Therefore, learning how to curate one's own digital footprint and use digital media to positively influence identity development are crucial elements of digital citizenship.

- **Relationships and communication.** As students enter their teenage years, they become more and more interested in their relationships. And today's teens use digital media to sustain, deepen, and, in some cases, *create* relationships. Social media, in particular, has been proven to make many teens feel more connected to each other. For some, however, social media may highlight the ways in which they are excluded. It's also important to note that texting has become more common than in-person conversation. All this points to the need for students to learn how to build positive relationships online.

- **Cyberbullying, digital drama, and hate speech.** By their teens, most students have experienced anything from mean-spirited comments to rumormongering to bullying online. Many of our students will be exposed to online hate speech (racism, sexism, homophobia, transphobia) at some point. Students must learn how and why to be kind and supportive online, and, conversely, how and why to avoid damaging online behavior.

- **News and media literacy.** The Common Sense report refers to "news and media literacy" — which, in Chapter 4, I refer to as information literacy and digital literacy, respectively. As I noted in that chapter, there is no consensus on what constitutes a literacy. There's certainly a level of interconnectedness to the literacies commonly described as such. Nevertheless, for our purposes here, just know that what I have described as information literacy and digital literacy are both important aspects of digital citizenship.

Global learning community

The global learning community refers to the network of learners all over the world. I find it helpful to frame the teaching and learning happening in our schools as part of the global learning community, as doing so prevents us from seeing our work with students as disconnected from the world outside. Indeed, we remember that our school is part of the world. This may seem self-evident, but for many it really is a paradigm shift.

When we intentionally connect our teaching and our students' learning with the global learning community, we look outside ourselves and our schools for ideas, resources, and inspiration. Our work — and our students' work — becomes imbued with a greater sense of significance. Education also becomes more exciting for everyone involved because there's a sense of genuine connection to the world, not just the world within one school.

As I said earlier, schools can feel like insular communities. Whenever and wherever this is the case, students (and teachers!) can feel as if their work is limited and even discriminatory. After all, if we're not looking beyond ourselves and our schools then we're very often closed off from a multiplicity of perspectives. For this reason, I would argue that we all have a mandate to make meaningful connections to the world beyond the walls of our classrooms and schools.

It's easy to understand why we don't do this enough. By and large, educators are asked to do too much and given too little time to do it all. However, framing one's self, one's class, and one's school as part of the global learning community can put teaching and learning into perspective. We begin to prioritize the elements of our jobs differently, with a greater emphasis on what makes our students and us feel more connected. And when students feel more connected, they're naturally more engaged.

The "global learning community" is referenced numerous times in the AASL Standards Framework for Learners — a framework that school librarians use to guide our work in schools. Because librarians work across grade levels and subject areas, these standards are applicable to most classroom settings. I'll share just a couple of specific standards here:

- "Learners contribute a balanced perspective when participating in a learning community by ... [describing] their understanding of cultural relevancy and placement within the global learning community."

- "Learners adjust their awareness of the global learning community by … [evaluating] a variety of perspectives during learning activities."[82]

You can see that these standards are intended to help us teach students that they're part of a worldwide network of learners — that they're part of something bigger than themselves. This is indeed the goal of facilitating their participation in the global learning community.

Building connections to the outside world

In this section, I want to clearly link "digital citizenship" with the "global learning community" and explain how both are essential to consider when working to build connections to the outside world.

First, I should note that both terms represent work that is in the 21st century school librarian's purview. We actively promote and teach digital citizenship in our work with K-12 students and, as you saw in the AASL Standards shared above, we help our students make direct connections between their work and the work of the global learning community.

Quite simply, students must study digital citizenship in order to safely and effectively participate in the global learning community. Without learning the digital citizenship essentials — media balance and wellbeing; privacy and security; digital footprint and identity; relationships and communication; cyberbullying, digital drama, and hate speech; and news and media literacy — students would have to try to navigate online connections without the scaffolding they need.

Students thrive when they feel like they're part of something bigger than themselves. They thrive when the learning they're doing in the classroom feels connected with life outside school. This is where our framing of our teaching and learning as part of the global learning community comes into play. When we position ourselves and our schools in this way, we become more likely to make more direct links between what's being taught and what's happening in the world right now. So, when we teach digital citizenship and emphasize our role within the global

---

82   American Association of School Librarians. (2018) *AASL Standards Framework for Learners*, American Library Association. https://standards.aasl.org/wp-content/uploads/2017/11/AASL-Standards-Framework-for-Learners-pamphlet.pdf

learning community, we help students build meaningful connections to the outside world.

Overcoming challenges

As 21st century educators, we have so many opportunities for connection outside our own schools. In *Leading From the Library*, Shannon McClintock Miller and William Bass put it this way: "As the digital world has expanded, so too has our community expanded beyond its geographical borders. This means we must strike a balance between our local community and our extended community."[83]

Although this expanded sense of community is exciting and accompanied by all sorts of opportunities, it also comes with its own challenges. Below, I'll outline a few that you might experience yourself as you work to build meaningful connections to the outside world. For each, I'll also share suggestions for how to overcome it.

Lack of ideas

You might feel motivated to begin making new connections to the outside world for your students, but be unsure of how and where to start. I get it. There are endless possibilities and that can be overwhelming. If you're feeling stuck, one of the best ways to move forward is to connect with an educator who is already helping to make great connections for their students. Find someone inside or outside your school who has experience in facilitating any of the following:

- Book clubs in which students from multiple schools participate.
- Service learning projects (if applicable, those related — even tangentially — to your content area).
- Pen-pal programs (visit www.penpalschools.com to start your own).
- Interviewing experts from outside the school.
- Author visits (in-person or virtual).
- Coding clubs in which students from multiple schools participate.

83   McClintock Miller, S. & Bass, W. (2019) *Leading from the Library: Help Your School Community Thrive in the Digital Age*, International Society for Technology in Education

- Visits to local museums, theaters, historical sites, businesses, etc.
- Collaborative projects with schools in the area (in-person or virtual).
- Student-created social media posts for school accounts.
- Using social media tools to connect students with the local and global communities.
- Blogs in which students from multiple schools post and comment.
- The Global Read Aloud (theglobalreadaloud.com).
- Audio or video projects that involve students connecting with others outside school (podcasts, films, etc.).
- Virtual debates in which students from multiple schools participate.
- Student-led environmental action programs that involve the community.
- Contests that involve multiple schools.
- Students publishing in newspapers or magazines.

You might notice that although many of these are digital or virtual options, several include in-person contact. As someone who doesn't love event planning (coordinating schedules, buses, emails, etc.), I can honestly say that each time I've done so, the experience has been worth it. Students love going beyond their standard routine, and the experience for me is often eye-opening and inspiring.

The list above is by no means exhaustive. It's my hope that at least one of the ideas listed above will sparked some possibilities for you, especially possibilities in which you might strengthen or deepen students' understanding of a topic you're already addressing.

Lack of time
We've discussed this as a challenge in previous chapters, because it's almost always a problem — if not *the* problem — for educators interested in starting something new. As I referenced in those earlier chapters, for me this really boils down to mindset. If what you're trying to do feels

important enough, or perhaps even essential, then of course you'll figure out ways to make it happen. In this case, I hope you're feeling a strong desire to help your students build meaningful connections to the outside world.

That said, I'd like to share the following list, "5 powerful ways to save time as a teacher,"[84] published by Jennifer Gonzalez on her popular education blog *Cult of Pedagogy* and based on a podcast conversation she had with Angela Watson. Hopefully this list will help you make that mindset shift from "I don't have time" to "I want and need to do this." Below, I share Watson's five tips for saving time, along with a brief summary of each.

1. **Eliminate unintentional breaks.** Put yourself in a position — mentally and ideally physically — in which you minimize in-person and digital distractions.

2. **Figure out the Main Thing and do it first.** What is the one thing you absolutely must do today? Do that thing first.

3. **Work ahead by batching and avoid multitasking unless the work is mindless.** Schedule specific times for certain tasks, such as checking and responding to email, and avoid frequently jumping back and forth between activities.

4. **Look for innovative ways to relax any standards that create unnecessary work.** Remember that you don't need to do everything and you don't need to be perfect. Where can you aim for good instead of great?

5. **Use scheduling to create boundaries around your time.** Build blocks of time in your schedule for certain tasks, using your best estimates for how long each task should take. You can adjust on the go, but simply having time built into your day can help maximize your efficiency.

Of course, I'm sharing these ideas in the specific context of finding time to figure out how to connect your students to the outside world. Therefore, if you're so inclined, use one or a few of them to bank yourself

---

84   Gonzalez, J. (2015) "5 powerful ways to save time as a teacher," *Cult of Pedagogy.* www.cultofpedagogy.com/40hour

some time for exploring new connection opportunities. The effort will be worth it.

Blocked social media

In *Connected Librarians*, Nikki D. Robertson details how and why librarians and other educators use social media in the classroom to connect students with the outside world. Using social media remains controversial in some schools and districts, though I don't believe it should be. From upper elementary to high school, our students use social media to communicate with their peers and others. If we want our work with students to feel relevant to the way they actually live their lives — and the way they will continue to live their lives in the future — then it follows that using social media for classroom learning is probably a good idea. The problem is that in many schools, social media sites are blocked. In her book, Robertson shares her response to school administrators blocking social media:

> *Fear and the desire to protect students often prevent administrators from conceptualizing social media as an integral part of our emerging, technology driven educational system. According to the National Education Technology Plan (NETP), various forms of social media use by students are viewed as not only essential, but commonplace, in today's schools (U.S. Department of Education, 2017). Social media tools give students a voice to communicate with mentors, peers, teachers, subject area experts, and more. Administrators whose vision falls short in imagining the possibilities for social media to enhance and personalize the educational experience for students are ultimately hindering deeper learning. They are also setting students up for failure once they leave the safety of school, and are culpable adults. Students need real-world experience where they can practice applying their knowledge.[85]*

Although she is writing for other school librarians, Robertson's recommendations for overcoming this challenge apply to other educators as well. Robertson argues that we should become familiar with what's

---

85   Robertson, N.D. (2018) *Connected Librarians: Tap Social Media to Enhance Professional Development and Student Learning*, ISTE

actually legal (if legality is being questioned), model the use of social media and share the results with our school and/or district, and if applicable do what we can to ease parents' anxieties. If you find yourself wanting to use social media as a means through which to connect your students to the outside world, I highly recommend Robertson's book as a primer. She discusses everything from blogs to hashtags to Snapchat, and it's a relatively short read.

School libraries leading the way

Because school librarians work across grade levels and subject areas, we don't have the same classroom boundaries as many other educators. This definitely influences how we often think beyond the boundaries of our schools, too. But as I mentioned earlier, it's actually part of our job to connect our students and schools with the global learning community. This is what today's school librarians do.

In my own role as librarian, I work with our parent library committee (a team of volunteers who generously help with various library-related tasks) to coordinate author visits for our school. This is, of course, a classic way to bring in voices from the outside world. Students love these opportunities to connect with real-world authors. That said, our author visits look a little different from the standard format, which typically has the author talking specifically about their book(s) for the bulk of their visit and facilitating some form of Q&A. I decided to take a different approach when I realized several years ago that teachers often don't have the time and flexibility to read the visiting author's book — especially if we're talking about middle-grade fiction, for example.

Instead of a traditional author visit, I ask that most of our visiting authors use their book as a vehicle to teach our students something about the writing process. This format has been quite successful across the grades (I work in a Pre-K–8 school) and in my mind it serves two crucial functions. First, the author still has the opportunity to talk about their book, build excitement about it, and share excerpts. And they still bring along signed copies for families to purchase. But the second function — sharing some part(s) of their writing process and teaching specific writing skills — is how these visits become even more impactful. This way, the author is able to address reading *and* writing skills, which helps our students and our teachers. I know I've learned a ton about writing from these visits.

These authors don't have to be "big names," either. Bringing in local (or relatively local) authors who write for children and/or teens is such a wonderful way to connect your students and your school as a whole with the local writing community. One author, who visited us several years ago, brought in some of the notebooks in which he writes his books by hand and shared that he does all his writing in the local public library. Details like these enable students to imagine themselves as writers, too.

Visits from authors, or any kind of professional whose work is related to something your students are studying, are immensely valuable experiences. Students see that what they're doing in school happens in the so-called real world, too. They can put a face and a story to that work, and they can begin to imagine themselves doing that work. Although this probably goes without saying, these visits can easily be facilitated virtually. And they're often faster and cheaper to facilitate this way! Today, so many more people are comfortable with interfaces such as Zoom, Skype, and Google Meet, which means it's easier than ever to make these kinds of connections to the outside world for your students — and perhaps even to make these connections commonplace.

In previous chapters I discussed the Passion Project, a weekly fifth-grade class I co-facilitate with our technology integrationist. This project has students executing an in-depth study of something they're interested in or passionate about. To my mind, one of the most important elements of this project is how we help connect students with adults who are experts about their topics. Sometimes these are adults in our school community — parents, educators, educators' spouses, etc. — but usually they're outside our school.

We brainstorm possible connections with each student and then support them to actually make those connections. We help them identify where to look for experts on their topic and how to find their contact information. We even look over the emails that students draft to the people that we've together determined to be good options. The idea is to have each student facilitate a short interview — via phone, Zoom, or email — in which they share the nature of their project and ask a few specific questions that we've discussed beforehand.

Although students aren't always able to find or successfully connect with an expert about their topic, those who do learn a lot about professional correspondence, asking good questions, and taking control over their own learning. Even the students who aren't able to successfully connect with an expert at the very least have their idea of research expanded. They learn that certain individuals can be sources of good information — and that personal anecdotes from experts and/or professionals can add color and depth to any kind of research project.

Connecting with experts helps students understand that their work is part of the global learning community — that they're directly connected to the world outside school. The stakes for their project become higher, too, because the stakes are real. This is one of the best ways I've come across to build student engagement and self-advocacy, and it can easily be applied to most subjects and grade levels, with the obvious caveat that lower grade levels will require a higher degree of teacher facilitation.

Forward-thinking librarians

As I mentioned earlier, teaching digital citizenship provides students with the skills they need to successfully navigate — and participate in — the global learning community. One potential problem with teaching digital citizenship is that it can be easy to fixate on telling students what *not* to do. This is especially true when we teach students about media balance, privacy and security, and digital footprint and identity. For this reason, I want to draw your attention to an educator who frames and teaches digital citizenship in a helpful, positive way — a way in which the emphasis is on *community*.

Dr. Kristen Mattson, a consultant who worked for years as a school librarian, is the author of *Digital Citizenship in Action*. In her introduction to the book, she frames her pedagogical stance as one rooted in possibility and mutuality:

Being able to connect globally offers a magnitude of possibilities for learning, collaborating, and even working together to change the world, but that means digital citizenship curricula must strive to show students possibilities over problems, opportunities over risks, and community successes over personal gain.[86]

Mattson writes that we must create opportunities for students to test new digital tools with each other, with scaffolding and support from teachers. We should also clearly articulate what it means to be a digital consumer and a digital creator by giving students opportunities to reflect on their own digital citizenship through these two distinct lenses. When we frame our teaching of digital citizenship as a way to teach students to exchange ideas in community with other people, the whole enterprise begins to feel more positive and community-oriented.

One particular approach of Mattson's is directly related to building and sustaining relationships with the outside world. Mattson emphasizes the power of teaching students to move beyond online personal branding — often a primary digital focus for middle and high school students — into creating and sustaining a networking mindset. With the networking mindset, students move from questions like "How can I get noticed?" and "How can I create an impressive 'look' and 'feel' to increase my followers?" to questions like "How can I become connected with a community?" and "What can I offer to the community?"[87] We can encourage students to use these latter questions to center the global community of learners when we're teaching almost any element of digital citizenship.

To begin the process of creating a networking mindset, Mattson recommends having students reflect on their own interests, identify what online communities might help them learn more about their interests, and consider how they could share their own experiences and ideas with others in those communities.[88] Once they've had some time to reflect and brainstorm, they will be empowered with new ideas and aware of new possibilities. In this way, digital citizenship becomes truly relational.

---

86   Mattson, K. (2017) *Digital Citizenship in Action: Empowering Students to Engage in Online Communities*, ISTE

87   Ibid.

88   Ibid.

After all, citizenship is nothing if not about how we're connected to other people.

Cindy Hundley is a school librarian at Gutermuth Elementary School in Louisville, Kentucky. She is passionate about helping her students make meaningful connections to the outside world. Hundley gave a presentation titled "Global connections, zero budget" at the 2019 AASL National Conference and below she shares with me some of the great initiatives in which she and her students have participated.

- **#ScratchPals**: "I have participated in this project for the past few years and am now a #ScratchPals ambassador," Hundley tells me. "I find this project to be an important one as kids get the opportunity to learn and practice coding skills, can provide and receive feedback, and meet others from around the world. My students like the project even though they are often challenged by the coding. Before we went virtual because of Covid-19, my students created virtual postcards for one of the Italian #ScratchPals groups as they had to withdraw because they were going virtual. My students were so engaged, empathetic, and kind to the Italian students and thought it was super-cool that they were sending their artwork to Italy!"

- **#GridPals** is another great program that comes highly recommended by Hundley. "It's a way for classes around the world to connect using the tools at Flipgrid," she says. "If teachers are interested, they add their information to the GridPals portion of the site and then search for other classes also interested or wait until another teacher approaches them in order to connect. The year I participated in the program, I connected with another teacher in Canada. He was a computer science teacher, and we had our students introduce themselves and share information about Louisville, Kentucky, while they shared about Canada. My students loved making friends with kids in Canada and enjoyed watching the videos they received."

- "**Students Rebuild** is a project that addresses a different global issue yearly and asks students to participate by creating a product that can then be used to raise funds supported by the

Bezos Foundation," Hundley tells me. "In years past, students learned about the plastic pollution problem affecting the oceans and then created ocean-themed art using recycled materials. Every piece of art that was created contributed $3 toward helping remove plastic pollution from the ocean. Students used recycled materials from our makerspace and showed such creativity. They were so proud of the money our school raised and they felt that they had made a difference in their world by their actions."

- "**#EpicPals** is a quick global connection created by Sara Malchow," Hundley says. "Each month, [Malchow] chooses six books from Epic for K-2 students and six books for [grades] 3-5 students based on a theme. She then creates a Padlet for students to use as a platform for a reading response. Students are encouraged to read and comment on the responses of others and to add their own. While this isn't a face-to-face project, students see that they can connect to others around the world based on a book. I enjoy this one as it ties in reading and writing as major components. It helps students in the lower grades understand that their words carry weight and that others want to hear what they have to say. It's a great intro to global connections for those wanting to start connecting with others worldwide."

These are just a few initiatives that Hundley's students participate in. "To be honest," she tells me, "once I started looking for global connection opportunities, I couldn't stop. I made it a professional growth goal that every student in our school [K-5] would make at least one global connection a year. The kids love the different activities and are always excited to make 'new friends.'"

Hundley believes that building these connections to the outside world helps students understand the many positive ways in which technology can be used to meet and work with other people safely and productively. And she notes that when students meet and/or work with peers from different parts of the world, they come to understand that they all have a lot in common. "I think in the world we live in, this is a crucial awareness," Hundley says. "Teaching kids to be tolerant of others may be one of my most important jobs. Making these global connections helps me do this in an effective and engaging way."

Ali Schilpp, school librarian at Northern Middle School in Accident, Maryland, was named *School Library Journal*'s School Librarian of the Year in 2018. In a blog post written for Scholastic, she details some of the impressive ways she has helped her students "go global." Here's her rationale for doing this work with her small-town students.

I knew the power of global citizenship from working in a large district and felt my students needed authentic connections. Moving to a small, rural community school gave me the incentive to seek out collaborations to provide "windows," opportunities to meet and observe diverse people, their culture and develop empathy. The greatest need is to provide "doors," an incentive to move beyond one location and seek opportunities, connections and adventures.[89]

For Schilpp, technology access should be the gateway to building meaningful connections to the outside world. She argues that this is how educators can successfully tie together digital citizenship and participation in the global learning community. She goes on to share some specific ways in which she engages her students in global learning opportunities, beginning with a project called #LegoTravelBuddy. Schilpp connects with teachers and librarians all over the world, shipping Lego's Travel Building Suitcase from one location to the next. Each new recipient shares pictures of the Lego set in its new location. Students then connect with each other about books, geography, and more through digital applications like Flipgrid.

On the next page are a few of Schilpp's other recommendations for building global connections, some of which I've summarized and some of which I've expanded upon.

89   Schilpp, A. (2019) "How 'going global' can support multiple literacies and digital citizenship," Scholastic. https://edublog.scholastic.com/post/how-going-global-can-support-multiple-literacies-and-digital-citizenship

- **Participate in the Scholastic Read-a-Palooza Summer Reading Challenge.** According to Scholastic, this "unites kids, parents, educators, public librarians, community partners, and booksellers in a nationwide campaign that celebrates reading for fun while improving access to books during the summer."[90]

- **Join www.bookcrossing.com,** a social networking site centered around books. Here's how it works: "Breath new life into books instead of letting your old favorites collect dust — pass them along to another reader. Our online archival and tracking system allows members to connect with other readers, journal and review literature, and trade and follow their books as lives are changed through 'reading and releasing.'"[91]

- **Connect with a global coding club** such as Code Club International (www.codeclubworld.org) or Girls Who Code (www.girlswhocode.com).

- **Watch Story Time from Space** with early elementary students. This is an initiative by the Global Space Education Foundation, a nonprofit organization that "[sends] children's books to the International Space Station … [where] astronauts are videotaping themselves reading these books to the children of Earth."[92]

- **Participate in the FIRST Lego League Challenge**, "an international research and robotics competition in which teams work in four challenging categories (Robot Game, Robot Design, Research, Core Values)."[93]

- **Join Fandom Forward**, which describes its mission in this way: "We use the power of story and popular culture to make activism accessible and sustainable. Through experiential training and real life campaigns, we develop compassionate, skillful leaders who learn to approach our world's problems with joy, creativity, and commitment to equity."[94]

90 www.scholastic.com/content/dam/scholastic/summerReadingChallenge/2020/pdfs/RAP_InfoSheet_English_200528.pdf
91 www.bookcrossing.com/about
92 https://storytimefromspace.com/about-us
93 www.first-lego-league.org/en
94 https://fandomforward.org/mission

As you can see, there are plenty of great connection-building options for all educators, regardless of what or whom you teach, or where you fall on the spectrum of experience. Schilpp and the other school librarians I've referenced in this section are all great models for how to do this important and exciting work of connecting our students to the outside world. In the next section, we'll look at how you can begin new initiatives at your school.

Takeaways for all educators

The beauty of building meaningful connections to the outside world for your students is that doing so allows you to build community. You build community in your classroom by involving everyone in something that's bigger than each of you as individuals. And you build community in a larger sense, too, because you become connected to the global learning community.

In this chapter, I've shared many ways that librarians and other educators have connected their students to the global learning community. But one of the best parts of this work of connection-building is that you can create any kind of opportunity that you want for your students. It all depends on who you are, who your students are, and what you'd like to accomplish.

In *The Art of Community*, Charles H. Vogl shares this note about building community:

> *There's no single formula. What works for you and your members [students] will not work for everyone. Success will reflect your values, priorities, and growth. Just as in art, there are forms and skills you can build on, but copying someone else won't create something truly inspiring. You have to bring your own creativity and experience to the work.*[95]

This isn't to say that you won't inspire your students by trying out any of the specific ideas shared in this chapter. Rather, it's an invitation to think of ways you could motivate and inspire your particular group(s) of students by connecting them to the outside world. You should absolutely

---

95   Vogl, C.H. (2016) *The Art of Community: Seven Principles for Belonging*, Berrett-Koehler

use any existing ideas or programs that would resonate with your students, and you can always make adjustments to suit their individual needs and interests.

If you're a teacher who's interested in beginning this work today, you might benefit from first connecting with whoever teaches digital citizenship in your school. Ask them what digital citizenship skills have already been taught to students in your grade level(s) and what kind of scaffolding they still need in order to participate in learning opportunities that involve connecting with the outside world. You might also consider reflecting on the extent to which you're teaching digital literacy in your classroom (see Chapter 4 for more on this). You'll need a good sense of what your students *still need to know* in order to be safe, successful, and empowered in making new online connections.

Next, take an inventory of the ideas shared in this chapter and/or any other ideas that have come to mind while reading. If you haven't already, begin thinking of specific places in your curriculum where you could implement the ideas that interest you the most and would likely interest your students, too. You could also survey your students: ask them where and how they would be most interested in connecting what they're learning in the classroom to the outside world. Whenever I pose questions like this to my students, I'm always impressed by their contributions.

Once you have a rough idea of where in your curriculum you'd like to create opportunities for your students to build meaningful connections to the outside world, you can begin making specific plans. You could connect with educators you know inside or outside school who have experience with this and can offer you practical advice. You might also need to be in touch with the people outside your school that your students are likely to contact and/or collaborate with. And don't forget to keep in mind those digital citizenship skills your students still need in order for you to successfully scaffold the project or unit you're planning to teach. You'll need to teach (or co-teach with an educator who specializes in digital citizenship) these skills on the front end and throughout the project or unit.

Once you're actively helping your students build meaningful connections to the outside world, do everything you can to share your initiative with your colleagues, administrators, and — if possible — with your professional learning network. There's a good chance you'll hear from others about opportunities for even more collaboration and connection-building. Plus, you'll inspire the educators around you to make these kinds of connections for their students, too. Good ideas are likely to spread, thereby making a positive impact on even more students.

Administrators, if you're interested in creating or expanding opportunities for connecting your students to the outside world, I suggest you start by highlighting any teachers who are already doing this work in your school. Have them share the nature of their project(s) at faculty meetings and how their students have benefitted from making meaningful connections with individuals and/or communities outside school. You might also connect with the educators in your building who are charged with teaching digital citizenship — typically school librarians and/or technology specialists. These educators can let you know to what extent students in each grade level have already learned fundamental digital citizenship skills. They can also work with you to develop over time a school-wide "networking mindset,"[96] as Dr. Kristen Mattson calls it, so that building meaningful connections to the outside world becomes a standard way of being at your school.

You might even say explicitly to your faculty that you want your school to "go global," and that you'll do everything you can to support them in this effort. When your school community has a common language and common philosophy around teaching digital citizenship and participating in the global learning community, you really can construct a culture in which your school sees itself as one important part of a greater whole. Imagine how much better prepared your students will be for our highly networked world if they leave your school having already built meaningful connections outside school through everyday classroom learning experiences. Plus, when your students build meaningful connections to the outside world, more people become aware of your school. All sorts of

---

96   Mattson, K. (2017) *Digital Citizenship in Action: Empowering Students to Engage in Online Communities*, ISTE

new opportunities tend to crop up. I've seen this at my school every time a colleague facilitates the building of new connections for and with their students: other educators learn about these initiatives and want to visit to learn more, and all sorts of new invitations are offered. As your school's participation with the outside world increases, so too the outside world becomes more interested in participating with your school.

How your librarian can help

School librarians teach digital citizenship and help students understand their place in the global learning community. An increasing number of us also follow the International Society for Technology in Education Standards, one of which is focused specifically on the community-oriented aspect of digital citizenship that we've talked a lot about in this chapter. According to that standard, we're tasked with "[creating] experiences for learners to make positive, socially responsible contributions and exhibit empathetic behavior online that builds relationships and community."[97]

Given our leadership in this area, here are some of the ways we can help teachers begin to make meaningful connections to the outside world for their students.

- **Researching, finding, and creating connections.** You're welcome to come to us and ask for advice on where and how you might facilitate these kinds of connections for your students. Tell us what you're teaching (or what you're planning to teach) and, based on how much support you want or need, we can research, find, and even help create connections for your students. We're often highly networked ourselves and might have a few good ideas right off the bat. But if not, we can absolutely do the work of identifying some good options that might work well for your particular class(es). We really enjoy helping in this way and we're generally quite flexible in terms of how involved you'd like us to be.

- **Teaching mini-lessons.** Once you have a good idea of how you'd like to proceed, you can ask us to visit your classroom — or, in many cases, you can bring your class(es) to the library — so we can take the lead in teaching digital citizenship skills

---

97   www.iste.org/standards/for-educators

that will help your students safely and effectively connect with the global learning community. If you'd prefer, we can drop into your classroom several times over the course of several weeks to teach short, interconnected mini-lessons — all through the lens of the networking mindset. Or you can come to the library, have us teach a lesson, and then stay there as you proceed with whatever else you have planned for the period(s). That way, we can be available to help with any questions that may arise, or even to work with students one-on-one or in small groups.

- **Co-facilitating.** If you'd like us to be more involved, there's a good chance that, if our schedule permits, we'll be able to help you co-facilitate connection-building lessons, units, or projects. Sometimes this kind of teaching collaboration develops organically through the planning process, and sometimes both parties articulate on the front end that this will be a teaching collaboration. Either way, we get excited about these kinds of opportunities because they allow us to integrate 21st century library skills into other curricula.

Administrators, we want to help you, too. You can tap us to lead any initiatives you have in mind that involve your school building connections to the outside world. Because we work with many different teachers and curricula, there's a good chance we know where there are ripe opportunities for making and/or strengthening these kinds of connections. As I've tried to make clear in this section, we really are eager to help teachers do this work for and with students. We know the benefits of helping students become good digital citizens, and we understand the possibilities that come along with awareness of — and active participation in — the global learning community. Even if your school has limited technological resources, there are many exciting possibilities for making your students feel more connected to the world around them. Let us know how we can help.

Reflecting on purpose

I'd like to close this chapter by briefly reflecting on "purpose." In the context of building connections to the outside world, I'd like to think about purpose in two distinct ways. First, the kind of connection-building that we've discussed throughout this chapter gives our students a clearer sense of purpose: why they're learning what they're learning. This is significant, as many of our students are still asking the question: *why do I need to know this?* When they're connected to the world outside their school, they see the topic's relevance firsthand. There's no longer that disconnect.

The second way I'm thinking about purpose is rooted in the two questions posed by Priya Parker in the beginning of her book *The Art of Gathering*: "The art of gathering begins with purpose: When should we gather? And why?"[98] As you think about ways to build meaningful connections to the outside world for your students, these two questions can keep you focused. Each of the specific guiding questions I share below are essentially offshoots of Parker's two framing questions.

Teachers:
- In terms of your curriculum, when would your students most benefit from connecting with the outside world?
- Why do you want your students to make this kind of connection? What specifically do you hope your students will learn?
- How could you give your students some choices in how they connect? What ideas do they have about this connection-building process?
- What are some specific ways your school librarian could help you in the beginning and/or during the process?

Administrators:
- To what extent is your school a global school?
- Which educators in your school are already building meaningful connections to the world outside? How can you highlight their work?
- What does your school's digital citizenship curriculum look like? Does it need to be reframed so that it's more about building connections and less about what students shouldn't do?
- How can your school librarian help with building these connections or increasing the number of them?

---

98   Parker, P. (2018) *The Art of Gathering: How We Meet and Why It Matters*, Penguin

Chapter 6
Revitalizing research

> "Research is formalized curiosity. It is poking and prying with a purpose"
> — **Zora Neale Hurston**

One of the most important things I've learned in my life is the importance of being curious. Whenever I'm open or eager to learn more, I'm inevitably led to new perspectives and possibilities. For me, this is part of what it means to live mindfully. It's about allowing myself to follow the questions, interests, and passions that occupy my thoughts and imagination, almost against my will.

Curiosity is what led me to make the career change from teaching English to being a school librarian. I really enjoyed teaching English. I had come to feel confident in my ability to do that job fairly well. But something inside me felt drawn to the work that I saw school librarians doing, from facilitating exciting school-wide initiatives to working with teachers and students in various grades and subject areas. I became curious about the job, researched it in different ways (including through conversations with school librarians), and ultimately took graduate courses toward school librarian certification.

Early in that process, I didn't expect my curiosity to lead me to actually changing careers. I wasn't certain that doing so was even a good idea. But the questions and possibilities in my head wouldn't go away. What's clear to me now, in my career as a school librarian, is that questions and possibilities are at the heart of what we call "research."

Teaching and facilitating research has long been a central responsibility of school librarians. We help students and teachers successfully navigate the overwhelming amount of information that is available almost instantaneously. As master curators, we teach effective curation and how to synthesize information from multiple sources. We facilitate the creative expression of what is learned throughout the research process. But most importantly, we give permission for students to trust and follow their curiosity — those questions that pop into their heads again and again.

Twenty-first century school librarians are leading the effort to revitalize the teaching of research in K-12 schools by centering students' curiosity. This is what we'll explore in detail throughout this chapter.

We'll begin by taking a close look at how research is framed and taught by many of today's school librarians, from students' initial inquiry process to the reflection that occurs at the end of assigned research projects. Education is more an art than a science, so each educator has their own unique approaches and processes. Different things work for different people. That said, it's my hope that this chapter will serve as a general blueprint for revitalized research in today's classrooms.

I'll also share some of the challenges you'll likely face when you begin to revitalize student research in your own work as an educator. Along with these challenges, I'll include some suggestions for overcoming them.

Next, I'll walk you through some real-world examples of what librarian-led (and co-led) research looks like in action inside today's school libraries and classrooms. The idea is to show you some of the innovative ways in which research is being facilitated and taught through school library curricula and programming.

I hope this chapter will support you to develop some new ideas for your own practice as an educator, no matter your grade level or discipline. I'll share some recommended takeaways for teachers and administrators alike, followed by a few guiding questions intended to get you thinking about how you might revitalize research in your classroom and/or school.

Blueprint for revitalized student research

Many of us were not taught to follow our curiosity. This is as true for educators as it is for any other adult. When we were students, research projects often weren't exciting prospects. I remember being assigned seemingly random topics to research, occasionally instructed on specific sources to use, and then asked to write a report with a bibliography. With few exceptions, this was dreadfully boring for me.

I don't want to project my past misgivings about research on to you. Perhaps you had teachers who were wonderful at teaching and facilitating research. However, I will venture to say that for the majority of us, research was a process that felt overwhelming, uninteresting, or a combination of the two. And I would argue that this was because our own curiosity wasn't prioritized or harnessed by our teachers.

Here's the thing: when we tap into students' curiosity, we not only help them access their own internal motivation, but we also help them better understand who they are. When we give them permission to inquire about questions, topics, and ideas that matter to them, we help them honor their desire to learn more about the world. And when they learn more about the world, they naturally learn more about their place within it.

Before you get started

Before anything else, I recommend that you pair up with your school librarian to discuss, plan, and even co-facilitate parts of the research process. School librarians can help you curate resources for your students, develop a solid plan for teaching research skills, and collaborate with you and your students throughout each stage of the research process. Whenever you start to think about an upcoming or new research project, come and talk to us. We want to help you.

As early as possible, start pulling together examples of good work from each part of the research process (good research questions, notes, thesis statements, bibliographies, final products, etc.) to share with your students. Ideally, you will also put together some examples yourself. This not only shows students your own investment in the research project you're about to undertake, but also gives you a better understanding of what it is exactly that you're asking them to do. Sharing your own writing and work with your students is good for any kind of assignment, and it's certainly useful with research because it shows students concrete, organized examples of what is often a messy process.

Whether they're examples you've created or examples from students you've taught in previous years, I cannot recommend enough providing examples for students to reference throughout the process — and regularly reminding them to look at these examples. When you roll out the project to your students, you can quickly show them what each step of the research process actually looks like and then do a deeper dive into each example, probably in the form of mini-lessons, when it's time to begin that part of the process.

Another important thing to remember before you get started is to give yourself and your students enough time for whatever research project you have in mind. If the process feels rushed, students are much less likely to engage with their topic in a meaningful way, and much more likely to regurgitate information instead of analyzing it. Plus, there's a very good chance that your students will need to learn (or review) specific research skills along the way. They'll need this scaffolding in order to do what you're asking them to do. This is another reason why working with your librarian can be beneficial.

I would also decide on what kind of flexibility you'd like to give your students in terms of how they share what they learn through their research. In other words, what will their final product look like? In *New Realms for Writing*, Michele Haiken offers many options for students to creatively express themselves. Below I list some of her ideas, each of which provides a stimulating opportunity for students to share their learning.

- Blend of personal narrative and research.
- Podcast.
- Multigenre project.
- Essay.
- Poetry (*Hamilton*-style raps, for example).
- Movie-making.

- Virtual reality.
- Makerspace projects.
- Film (documentary-style, especially).
- TED-style talks.
- Personal narrative.
- Speech.
- Blogs.[99]

Hopefully, just reading through this list gave you an idea or even multiple ideas. Once you've determined how students will be able to share their learning, you'll need to figure out their audience. I've enlisted students in this part of the process before (after introducing the general parameters of the research project) and they always have great ideas.

Not all their ideas will be possible, of course, but there's a good chance some of them will be. Involving them in the decision-making process early on shows you care about their contributions, which is central to revitalizing research. Plus, when students know their work will be shared with a real audience, it legitimizes the whole research process and this definitely raises the stakes for them.

You'll also need to decide whether to give your students a list of topics to choose from or ask them to consider their own. I've done both, and I can assure you that the latter requires much more time and can be much more difficult for many students. More one-on-one discussions are necessary and you run the risk of spending too much time on that part of the process. I do allow my fifth-graders to come up with their own topics, but that process is part of a year-long research project.

If you develop the list of topics yourself, you have the advantage of determining which topics are actually viable in terms of students' ability to access a variety of age-appropriate resources. Although this takes a lot more time for you on the front end, once your students have decided which topic they're most interested in they'll be ready to dive right in and start the inquiry process.

---

99   Haiken, M. (2019) *New Realms for Writing: Inspire Student Expression with Digital Age Formats*, ISTE

Framing the research project

Once you know the size, scope, and specifics of the research project, you're ready to introduce it to your students. I think about this as *framing* it for them because, as you know, the way a new lesson, unit, or project is framed can make or break it. If you pitch the project with enthusiasm and explain that you want students to follow their natural curiosity, they are much more likely to be interested in the whole endeavor.

Begin by noting that this is an exciting opportunity for students to follow their curiosity. What are they genuinely interested in learning more about? How does what they learn throughout the research process relate to them, their families, and/or their friends? Stress that students will be able to learn something new about their topics and themselves, and create new contributions to the global learning community through the process. (See Chapter 5 for more about connecting with the global learning community.)

Explain to your students that the research project is also a chance to be creative. When you introduce the unconventional option(s) for how they will share their learning at the end of the process, you'll immediately stoke their curiosity and imagination. Tell them that they will be given time to make sense of what they learn through their research and share their own informed take on some aspect(s) of the topic. In *It's a Matter of Fact*, Angie Miller puts it like this: "Anybody can look up facts, and anybody can report those facts back ... Research is a matter of making meaning from those facts. It's a matter of crafting intelligent responses and new ideas from facts. It's a matter of creating knowledge."[100]

You might even consider recommending that your students multitask a bit — to think *while they're researching* about how they might share their learning in innovative ways. I always tell my students to jot down ideas as they come to them, because they will inevitably forget them, as I do when I don't write my thoughts down.

You could add that the purpose of their final product — whatever it is — will be to inform and entertain their audience. I always say that if you're

---

[100]   Miller, A. (2018) *It's a Matter of Fact: Teaching Students Research Skills in Today's Information-Packed World*, Routledge

not enjoying what you're putting together then your audience probably won't enjoy it either. Again, it's all about following curiosity and being genuinely engaged with the work. When your students hear this message, they'll be much more eager to get started.

Beginning the inquiry process

At the very beginning of the research process, I recommend that you teach students how to cite their sources. MLA format[101] is most commonly used in K-12 schools, so that's what I teach. I'm honest about the fact that this is not a riveting part of the research process, but I tell my students that it's important to give credit where credit is due.

I also tell them that citing sources is a way of participating in the global learning community. It's a really cool way of personally responding to the published work of others and it lends credibility to students' own work — provided that the sources are reliable and applicable, of course. After all, any good research project proves or illustrates something new about the topic, and it's a great thing if students can find experts in the global learning community whose thoughts and ideas (arguably) support their arguments.

Once students have selected their topics and are ready to launch, I direct them to online encyclopedias, including Britannica and Wikipedia. The point is to take a bird's-eye view of their topic — or important elements of their topic — before they get to the nitty-gritty. Despite the fact that anyone can edit a Wikipedia entry, it's generally pretty reliable. But just in case, I ask students not to cite Wikipedia as a source. I show them that each Wikipedia article has its own sources at the bottom of the page, several of which might be good resources for their project.

Equipped with a general understanding of their assigned topics, students can begin to develop their own research questions. I recommend telling students that the idea here is to give their research a greater sense of focus. Given that you're asking them to follow their curiosity, their questions should be based on what they actually want to learn more about. In *Love the Questions*, Cathy Fraser notes that students should create "questions based on reading and connecting information to what

---

101   https://style.mla.org/mla-format

he or she [sic] already knows." Then, Fraser adds, students can determine "what sources will yield the best information for his or her [sic] study and [use] selected key search terms to locate information."[102] With this approach to inquiry, students are much more likely to be engaged and motivated to learn more.

Finding good information

The first step toward finding good information is bringing your class to the school library. It's pretty much guaranteed that you and your students will find having class in the library is a worthwhile experience, especially if you schedule a time with your librarian so they can be present or explicitly on hand to help. Librarians are master curators and finding good information is the process of curating resources.

Tell your students that they are not obligated to use information they do not find interesting. Their primary job during the research process is to follow their curiosity and reminding them of this is an important part of your facilitation of their work. If your librarian is helping, they can teach or co-teach specific ways for students to find good information. In terms of how to find helpful sources, here are the essentials that I teach.

- Use **academic databases**, which I define as large collections of information put together by experts and organized for you to search. I'm clear with students that databases are not sources themselves, in the same way that Google is not a source. Databases help us *find* sources. Then I show them how to access the databases that we make available through our school, with particular emphasis on the ones that are most relevant to their research project.

- Use **carefully scrutinized websites**. I ask students to consider who wrote whatever it is they're looking at and whether or not that person is an expert. I ask them to make sure they're clear about whether the information is fact-based or opinion. I ask them where it is coming from — a person? A school? A museum? And I ask them if what they're looking at cites *other* sources.

---

102   Fraser, C. (2018) *Love the Questions: Reclaiming Research with Curiosity and Passion*, Stenhouse

- Use **library books or library e-books**. If students are in the library, I will remind them where the nonfiction books are located and quickly review how to search the library catalog for specific titles. I'll also remind them about the various e-book options. I ask students to bookmark the library website, if they haven't already, because this site contains the search bar for our catalog and links to our e-book providers.

For academic databases, students will need some instruction on the use of keywords. They cannot simply type their questions into a database, as many of them do when they use Google. Once students know their topics and have drafted research questions, you can have them create word webs. They take a sheet of paper, write their research topic in the middle, circle the topic, and then around the circle write down the essential phrases, words, and/or concepts associated with their topics. Each new word written outside the circle functions as its own keyword. I recommend preparing a model beforehand to share with students. Word webs are a simple but effective way to help students begin the research process with a list of keywords that will allow them to search databases effectively.

When students use Google or other search engines, you can also teach them about Boolean operators. Here's an overview of their purpose from MIT Libraries.

- "They connect your search words together to either narrow or broaden your set of results."
- "The three basic Boolean operators are: AND, OR, and NOT."[103]

Google automatically adds "AND" to your multi-word searches. "OR" can be used to couple two related search terms. "NOT" will cut out any specific words that you don't want to appear in your search results. Including - (the minus sign) functions in the same way as adding "NOT" before the word you don't want in your results. Depending on their grade level, students may already be aware of these tricks. But for most research projects a quick review is probably in order, because Boolean operators can help students be much more efficient when using search engines. It's useful to model this by doing a live search in which you successfully broaden or narrow the results.

---

103   https://libguides.mit.edu/c.php?g=175963&p=1158594

Another crucial element to teach near the beginning of the research process is how to assess the credibility of any source found online. I share with my students these excellent and comprehensive questions from the University of California's Berkeley Library:

- **"Authority.** Who is the author? What is their point of view?"
- **"Purpose.** Why was the source created? Who is the intended audience?"
- **"Publication and format.** Where was it published? In what medium?"
- **"Relevance.** How is it relevant to your research? What is its scope?"
- **"Date of publication.** When was it written? Has it been updated?"
- **"Documentation.** Did they cite their sources? Who did they cite?"[104]

After I share these, I ask my students why these questions are important. It takes some time, but having them verbalize for each other the rationale for considering each of these questions is absolutely worthwhile. And if we're really trying to allow students to follow their natural curiosity, we should permit our older (middle and high school) students to use "the apps and information sources they employ outside of school as potentially cited resources in school," as Jennifer LaGarde and Darren Hudgins argue in *Fact vs. Fiction*:

> *What's the danger in letting students cite a Snap, Tweet, or Instagram post if we've emphasized fact checking as part of the research process? If we really want our students to apply a healthy level of skepticism to all information both in and out of school, we need to remove any barrier that prevents them from seeing how the skills we require they demonstrate during instruction apply even when their teachers are not around.*[105]

104 https://guides.lib.berkeley.edu/c.php?g=83917&p=539735
105 LaGarde, J. & Hudgins, D. (2018) *Fact vs. Fiction: Teaching Critical Thinking Skills in the Age of Fake News*, ISTE

Once students have found and scrutinized the resources they'd like to use, they can begin the note-taking process. I often have my students use simple Google Docs note templates because they can include hyperlinks to the sources they find, which makes them easy to revisit later if necessary. Our middle school students use the Cornell Notes system, in which the note-taking page is divided into two columns, with the topics/themes written or typed in the left-hand column and the notes themselves written or typed in the right-hand column. Summaries and/or reflections are included at the bottom of the page. It's a straightforward system that many high schools use, but I've used it successfully with upper elementary students as well.

Whatever note-taking system your students use, remind them regularly to keep their notes focused on their research question(s), with an eye toward what their thesis (overarching argument) might be. They don't need to take notes on details they learn about their topic that aren't directly related to the question(s) they're exploring. This will save them time and prevent them from including irrelevant or unhelpful details about their topic in their final product.

The other skill that needs to be explicitly taught and/or reviewed is how to avoid plagiarism. Plagiarism.org helpfully points out that each of the following is considered plagiarism:

- "Turning in someone else's work as your own."
- "Copying words or ideas from someone else without giving credit."
- "Failing to put a quotation in quotation marks."
- "Giving incorrect information about the source of a quotation."
- "Changing words but copying the sentence structure of a source without giving credit."
- "Copying so many words or ideas from a source that it makes up the majority of your work, whether you give credit or not."[106]

I suggest sharing this list with your students and telling them that the easiest way to avoid plagiarism is to correctly cite each source they use.

---

106 https://plagiarism.org/article/what-is-plagiarism

I highly recommend visiting Plagiarism.org yourself for a refresher on exactly what constitutes plagiarism and how to help your students avoid it.

Finally, I encourage you to urge your students to use a variety of different sources. With varied sources, they will be more likely to incorporate a diversity of viewpoints and gain a broader understanding of their topic. Therefore, they will be more likely to shift away from subjectivity and toward objectivity. Most academic databases allow you to choose "source types" (newspaper articles, encyclopedia entries, etc.), which is an easy way for students to begin to intentionally diversify their sources.

Synthesizing information

When students have curated information from a variety of good sources, they're ready to develop their own thoughts about their topic. Their research questions will have guided them to this point. Now they need help in synthesizing the information they've curated.

There are many ways to go about this. Some librarians and teachers ask students to use what's called a synthesis matrix. The Writing Center at the University of Arizona defines a synthesis matrix in this way:

> *A synthesis matrix is a table that can be used to organize research. When completed, it provides a visual representation of main ideas found in the [sources] and also shows where there is overlap in ideas between authors. A completed matrix will help to integrate all of the different resources together, which will facilitate the synthesis of information on a specific topic.*[107]

In terms of what the matrix actually looks like, "the sources are listed in the left column of the table, and the main ideas or themes about the topic are listed along the top of the table."[108] This way, students are able to create a visual of which main ideas or themes show up in the majority of their sources.

Regardless of whether or not you use a synthesis matrix, I can't recommend enough that you schedule time — at least a few minutes — to chat with

---

107   https://writingcenter.uagc.edu/synthesis-matrix
108   Ibid.

each student one-on-one. Students should be working independently during class periods, so hopefully you will have opportunities to talk with each of them about their ideas, how they're synthesizing them, and what their thesis statements might be. This is another opportunity to involve your school librarian. The two of you can set a timer for each conversation, and together you'll be able to cover twice as many students as you would on your own.

When students are ready to begin developing their own thesis statements (original arguments), they will need to focus on adding something new to the global conversation about their topic. This doesn't need to be daunting. You can tell your students that everybody has a different way of seeing the world, and therefore everybody will have different ideas about any given topic. Creating a thesis is a chance for each student to share their unique point of view.

The Writing Center at the University of North Carolina notes that a good thesis functions as a "demonstration of your ability to use or apply the material in ways that go beyond what you have read or heard."[109] The key here is going "beyond." As I mentioned earlier, this is an opportunity for students to be creative — to *create* new information about their topic. A new "take" on their topic, if you will.

This is difficult to do. I recommend that you start by teaching a lesson on what constitutes a good thesis statement. I tell my students that a thesis statement should be:

- **Arguable.** This means it can be debated. If your thesis is self-evident then there's no point in arguing it.
- **Provable.** There should be plenty of evidence in your research to support your argument.
- **One sentence long.** This makes your thesis easy to remember and share with others when you're talking about your research project.

Crucially, you should share some examples of good thesis statements. As with the other models you share, these can be thesis statements that

---

109 https://writingcenter.unc.edu/tips-and-tools/argument

you've created, or good examples from students in previous classes. Either way, I cannot stress enough the importance of this step. Students really do need to see examples of effective thesis statements. And they need the opportunity to articulate exactly what it is that makes them arguable and provable. All this can be covered in a single mini-lesson.

Still, you'll want to actually talk with them about their specific thesis statements. I recommend having them draft their theses before you meet with them. Let them know that these drafts are just that — *drafts*. There's a good chance that they will be revised when you chat with students and as they continue working. But at the very least these drafts provide starting points for your conversations with each other.

After the one-on-one discussions about thesis statements, which are basically short writing conferences, I ask students to revise the statements and share their new versions with me electronically. It's invaluable to create and keep a digital checklist of which students have had their thesis approved by me (and/or the colleagues with whom I'm collaborating). This way, I know exactly who needs a follow-up and who is ready to roll.

Sharing learning

Once students have synthesized the information discovered through the research process and developed a solid thesis, they're ready to begin working on their final product. As I mentioned earlier, there are lots of options you can share with your students to inspire them to articulate their argument creatively.

As long as the options you give them actually exist in the world outside school (podcasts, blogs, TED talks, etc.) then you will have provided them with invigorating learning opportunities. Students will not only learn how to express their arguments clearly and persuasively, but they'll also gain valuable practice in using real-world mediums that amplify their ideas in engaging and authentic ways.

Of course, you need to give your students a deadline for their final products. And if you've given them the freedom to choose from a list of different options, there's a good chance some of them won't be completely finished in time. I would argue that this is OK: the process is more important than the product. Those students can share their work-in-progress, explaining what their next steps would be and perhaps reflecting on how they might adjust their process next time. If you're grading students on their research project then I recommend giving more weight to their work during the process (you can regularly review their notes, outlines, thesis proposals, works cited, etc.) than their final product.

It's crucial to have a real-world audience for students' work. Whether you and your teaching collaborators host an in-person event for families or create a virtual exhibit to be shared with folks beyond your school community, your students will delight in the opportunity to share what they've learned and created.

Reflecting

If a research project is going to be repeated, it must evolve. The question of *how* can be answered by the students who actually go through the process. I often work with students and teachers on research projects that last more than just a few days or a week, so the projects are quite complex. Because of the many moving parts, when the process is finished it's easy to miss certain things and/or forget the lessons learned along the way.

I've found that sending out a Google Form survey is a great way to garner helpful feedback that I can easily return to before beginning the project with a new class. Here are some of the questions I've included on this type of survey.

- Did you enjoy working on this project? (Answer options: yes; no; kind of.)
- Please explain your answer to the previous question.
- What was the most enjoyable part of the process for you? Why was it enjoyable?
- What was the least enjoyable part of the process for you? Why was it not enjoyable?
- Which part of your project are you most proud of? Why?
- What two changes would you recommend that we make to this project next year?
- Do you have any suggestions for how we can best share your work with our school community?

- Are there any other thoughts about this project that you'd like to share?

Taken as a whole, students' responses illuminate which parts of the research project need to be revised so we can set up the next group of students for success. Google Forms make this process efficient — you can even have the responses sent to a single spreadsheet for easy reference later.

Overcoming challenges

No matter how prepared we are or confident in our own efforts to revitalize research for our students, we are sure to come across challenges. Trying something new and/or different means there will be a learning curve. The more we expect challenges, the better prepared we will be to take it easy on ourselves and calmly do what we can to overcome them.

Here are a few specific challenges you might face as you work to revitalize the research process. For each challenge, I've included a recommendation for how to overcome it.

Time constraints

In the research project blueprint shared over the previous sections, I noted that you'll want to give yourself enough time to teach (or review) important research skills and to allow students to move through each part of the process successfully. To those who feel a research project like this would require too much time, I would say that you can scale it up and down according to your needs — within reason, of course. Even for a mini research project, you'll need at least a week to facilitate the research process itself and a week for students to create and share their final products.

The good news is that you'll be teaching multiple literacies in the process. (See Chapter 4 for more on teaching multiple literacies.) So, if you're struggling with whether or not to devote time to a revitalized research project, keep in mind that not only will students be conducting in-depth studies, but they'll also be practicing and learning numerous important skills that are transferable to other subjects. Look for ways to incorporate the teaching of skills you usually teach in other units. Hopefully this will help you feel better about giving your students the time they need to follow their curiosity.

Level of complexity

Perhaps you're feeling overwhelmed by the blueprint I've shared with you. I get it. If more information is helpful, I recommend picking up one or more of the books I've mentioned in the previous sections:

- *Love the Questions* by Cathy Fraser.[110]
- *It's a Matter of Fact* by Angie Miller.[111]
- *Fact vs. Fiction* by Jennifer LaGarde and Darren Hudgins.[112]
- *New Realms for Writing* by Michele Haiken.[113]

Although each book takes a different approach and serves different purposes, all can help you flesh out the ideas and approaches that I've discussed. And rest assured that complexity is a good thing, especially for your students. You can teach the essential research skills one at a time, without devoting too much time to any of them. And you can reinforce those skills by chatting with students one-on-one as they work independently. Always remember the ever-available option of collaborating with your school librarian. We can help you at each stage of the research process, making teaching and facilitating a revitalized research process feel much less daunting.

Concerns about rigor

For some teachers and administrators, new approaches to teaching and learning are questioned right out of the gate, often with the assumption that creative approaches won't lead to real learning. I want to be clear that giving your students non-traditional options for making their arguments does not mean less rigor. In fact, moving away from traditional research papers and toward research led by innate curiosity will very likely mean your students bring more of themselves to the process and want to work harder. Many of them, especially middle and high school students, are so

---

110 Fraser, C. (2018) *Love the Questions: Reclaiming Research with Curiosity and Passion*, Stenhouse

111 Miller, A. (2018) *It's a Matter of Fact: Teaching Students Research Skills in Today's Information-Packed World*, Routledge

112 LaGarde, J. & Hudgins, D. (2018) *Fact vs. Fiction: Teaching Critical Thinking Skills in the Age of Fake News*, ISTE

113 Haiken, M. (2019) *New Realms for Writing: Inspire Student Expression with Digital Age Formats*, ISTE

accustomed to cranking out traditional research papers — often without genuine curiosity or interest — that just the novelty of taking a different approach will require them to think and work in new ways.

School libraries leading the way

In my own work as a school librarian, one specific way that I've successfully revitalized the research process is by teaching narrative writing that incorporates research. I've done this in both upper elementary and middle school, most recently with fourth-graders.

First, I work with the fourth-grade teachers to choose a list of topics for students to choose from. Then I tell students that they will research their topic and write fictional narratives that embed facts from their research. With this approach, students learn the elements of fiction and the research process simultaneously.

I try to set clear expectations about the dual purposes of this project: students need to find lots of facts about their topic and incorporate those facts into a short work of fiction. Students are often inspired by story-writing because so many ideas come to them during the research process. I set a low word limit for the short story and require students to include a set number of facts within it. For example, when I facilitate this kind of project with middle school students, I set a maximum word count of 750 and I require a minimum of 20 interesting facts from their research.

Essentially, this project means students have ongoing, built-in writing prompts. For example, if a student is researching orcas and comes across the fact that orcas can jump out of the water to snatch penguins or seals, they might be inspired to write an exciting — and true to life — penguin-snatching scene in their story.

Once students know the specific expectations, they begin the research process. A few mini-lessons about research can help them set the parameters of their work. I talk with students about how to find good sources, why it's important to use a variety of sources, and how to use keywords. Even if these lessons are just reminders, students will have a clearer sense of how to be efficient.

If the class I'm working with doesn't already have a note-taking system in place, I introduce one. For younger students, a mini-lesson on paraphrasing is often in order. I ask students to paraphrase the relevant information they find during the research process in bulleted form, with each bit of information they find functioning as a "fact" they can use in their story. After each fact, I ask them to include their source in parentheses — hyperlinked, if possible.

About halfway through the research process, students begin drafting their stories. This is when I make the transition from mini-lessons on researching to mini-lessons on writing short fiction. Students can alternate days of research and writing, or they can split the period and do research for half and writing for half. The first fiction mini-lesson typically involves sharing and discussing an age-appropriate example of "flash fiction," in which the author tells a compelling story with a satisfying ending in very few words. I tend to prioritize mini-lessons on creating and sustaining conflict, applying various methods of characterization, and using their authentic voice.

I discourage students from writing non-endings like "To be continued" or "It was all a dream!" because these avoid the difficult work of crafting a complete story. I ask them to imagine they are the reader and not the writer of their story: would they find the ending satisfying?

Most important, students must find creative ways to embed facts into their story. As they write, they underline or highlight the facts they've included. I try to help them find ways to sneak the facts into their story. For example, if a student is researching the geography of a state, they could use specific geographic features to describe the setting in the narrative.

When I need to assess or co-assess the projects, I ask students to submit their stories as well as their research notes. I use a simple rubric that includes all the skills from the mini-lessons, such as paraphrasing, source citing, and characterization. When the projects are complete, I often organize a listening party — an easy way to provide a real audience. I encourage students to listen on two levels: to enjoy the stories as stories and to identify the facts within them.

Whenever we successfully tap into students' creativity, they naturally become more curious. And they see that they really do have interesting stories to tell.

Forward-thinking librarians

Christine Ciofolo, librarian at Highlands Middle School in White Plains, New York, works directly with teachers to facilitate a research project called the Human Rights Museum. Ciofolo tells me she has helped cultivate this project for more than six years and it has been consistently successful.

First, students research the UN's Universal Declaration of Human Rights. "They choose one of the rights to work on with a group and then do research on that right," Ciofolo says. "Their final project is a hands-on, three-dimensional museum exhibit built only from recycled or household materials — much like a science fair project. Teachers then invite the community in to view the 'museum' and students act as docents explaining their human right, artifacts, and displays. As part of the exhibit, students often create guessing games or replicate some celebration or violation of that right. Some go further with a call to action supporting a cause or promoting awareness."

Ciofolo notes that her involvement with this research project has evolved over the years. "At first the teachers only wanted to give the students links to articles," she says. "After some discussion, we moved to using databases and news sources for research. I then volunteered the library as not only a research lab but a workshop for building and a space for displaying the museum artifacts. Because of the size of our library we were able to fit two or three classes of students in at the same time. The buzz was wonderful!"

In terms of student curiosity, Ciofolo says it builds slowly during this project. "They start by reading *A Long Walk to Water* by Linda Sue Park, then move on to view some documentaries, and finally are introduced to the UN Declaration of Human Rights," she explains. "They are always struck by how things are 'not fair,' which is very much a middle school-appropriate mindset." These narratives help pique students' curiosity, to say the least.

Takeaways for all educators

According to *Library Journal* and *School Library Journal*, students are entering college without the skills they need to successfully conduct their own research processes:

> *[A Library Journal] survey of more than 500 college librarians showed that students have trouble picking a research topic and creating objectives. They also rely heavily on Google searches; are overconfident about their research abilities; have trouble vetting sources for reliability; and can't properly cite sources.*[114]

Given this problem, K-12 educators must work together to help students learn the research skills they need. The more opportunities we can give students to hone their research skills, the better. After all, these skills will help them not only in college but also beyond. Let's be honest: you don't have to look very far to find examples of adults who have trouble finding reliable information and discerning between facts and opinions.

Whenever we facilitate research in the classroom, we have to keep in mind the importance of encouraging students to follow their innate curiosity. So much of schooling today involves educators telling students what's important, rather than giving students space to reflect on — and dig into — what *they* think is important.

Teachers, if you're interested in facilitating a revitalized research project, I recommend that you first consider the elements of your curriculum about which your students are most naturally curious. You know what I'm referring to — those topics that you don't have to frame or pitch with much effort before students begin asking all sorts of good, genuine questions. Then you can use the blueprint provided in this chapter to map out what a research project might look like around those specific topics.

---

114   D'Orio, W. (2019) "Lacking research skills, students struggle. School librarians can help solve the college readiness gap," *School Library Journal*, www.slj.com/lacking-research-skills-students-struggle-school-librarians-solve-college-readiness-gap-information-literacy

Strike up conversations with other educators who have taken more innovative or interesting approaches to student research. Ask them what worked and what didn't for their students and for them. Take notes. Explain exactly what you're up to: trying to facilitate a research project that capitalizes on students' innate curiosity and gives them creative options for sharing their work at the end of the process. Solicit feedback on your ideas and/or plans, and if appropriate ask them to help you out during the research project itself. This could look like anything from guest-teaching a mini-lesson on effective note-taking to assisting with one-on-one writing workshops on thesis statements.

Administrators, given *Library Journal*'s findings about how college students are often unprepared for college-level research, I highly recommend that you conduct some form of inventory of where research projects happen in your school and what they look like. Just as I've encouraged educators to do with students in this chapter, I would urge you to lead with genuine curiosity. Ask teachers what kinds of projects they're doing and the ways in which they're capitalizing on students' natural curiosity throughout the research process. Once you get a sense of what's happening and what's not happening, you can begin to think of ways to highlight examples of student research projects that are curiosity-based, and involve final products that extend beyond traditional research papers and are shared with a real audience. Any way you can find to celebrate this kind of student research project will go a long way toward creating a revitalized research culture in your school or district.

How your librarian can help

In *The Many Faces of School Library Leadership*, Violet Harada et al. note that school librarians are particularly well suited to facilitating the student inquiry process:

> *They may not be experts in every single curriculum area, but they are uniquely situated to gain a critical overview of the entire curricular landscape. They possess special expertise in the inquiry process and how research fits into that process. This expertise makes them "indispensable partners on learning teams" (Kuhlthau, Maniotes, and Caspari 2007, 16). They design activities to bridge the gap between theory and practice and*

provide the "holistic glue" that makes exercises relevant and authentic (Cropley 2014, 26).[115]

Because of this expertise, we can help you revitalize any existing research projects you currently facilitate, and/or develop an entirely new research project centered around student curiosity and inquiry. Below are some specific ways that we can be of assistance.

- **Developing a list of topics.** In the revitalized research blueprint shared at the beginning of this chapter, I mentioned the importance of setting your students up for success by allowing them to choose from a list of topics that have been vetted by you. Putting together such a list can be a time-consuming task, given that it involves a certain level of research to confirm that each topic is viable — that a variety of accessible, age-appropriate information is available. We can work with you to put together this list if you give us enough of a heads-up. This can save you a ton of time and potentially set you up for further assistance or collaboration.

- **Co-planning.** Helping you develop a list of research topics is absolutely a way of co-planning with you, but we can also help you map out even more of your revitalized research project. Just share what you have in mind, schedule a meeting with us, and approach the meeting with a collaborative (rather than delegative) spirit. A free-flowing brainstorming session will likely yield some exciting concrete results.

- **Teaching or co-teaching research skills.** Although teaching or co-teaching often results from earlier involvement in the research-project planning process, it doesn't have to. If you've already put together a solid plan but would like some assistance with teaching or co-teaching certain research skills, we're game. Just be clear with us about what you're hoping we can teach or co-teach, and give us enough time to put together lesson plans that are specific to your students' needs for your project. We can

---

115 Harada, V. with Ezaki Chun, L., Louis, P. & Okemura, A. (2017) "Librarians as learning leaders: cultivating cultures of inquiry," in Coatney, S. & Harada, V. *The Many Faces of School Library Leadership* (second edition), Libraries Unlimited

drop in for a single lesson, or we can make multiple visits over the course of several days or weeks. We can also assist you with writing workshops at various points throughout the research process.

- **Providing the school library as a workspace.** This option can be in addition to teaching or co-teaching with you. Any time students are working on research it's helpful for them to use the library as a workspace. They can spread out and have easy access to all the resources available throughout the school library. Some schools have a formal scheduling system for using the library as a classroom space; in other schools bookings are made through direct communication with the librarian(s). However you make the arrangements, you can ask the school librarian to be available to answer questions and provide support to students in the research process.

Administrators, we can help you make a case to faculty for revitalized research in your school. We care a lot about this topic and research is one of our essential areas of expertise. From leading in-school workshops on revitalized research to working with you to organically change the nature of student research in your school, we are ready and willing to take on this important leadership role. You might also consider reflecting on how revitalized research in your school can create opportunities for hands-on learning that addresses real-world problems (Chapter 1), prioritize the teaching of multiple literacies (Chapter 4), and build meaningful connections to the outside world (Chapter 5). These elements are interconnected, and their intersections are ripe with potential for innovative teaching and learning.

Formalized curiosity

In this chapter's epigraph, Zora Neale Hurston argues that "research is formalized curiosity." Indeed, as I've sought to argue, research projects in today's K-12 schools should be rooted in students' curiosity. I've provided a school librarian-inspired blueprint for how the research process can be "formalized." Now, to help you think more specifically about what revitalized research might look like in your classroom, department, school, or district, here are a few guiding questions.

Teachers:

- Can you identify one place in your curriculum that would benefit from a revitalized research project?
- What is the first step you could take toward planning a revitalized research project for your students? What is the second step?
- To what extent would it be helpful to involve your school librarian in the planning and/or facilitation of this project?
- How might you solicit ideas and/or feedback from your students to ensure that you stay focused on their needs and interests?

Administrators:

- If you ask a variety of students in your school or district their honest opinions about research, what do they say?
- Can you think of a few examples of research projects in your school or district that lead with students' curiosity and involve innovative final products that are shared with real audiences? If so, how can you highlight these projects and encourage other faculty to take a similar approach? If not, how can you share your vision with faculty?
- How can you help empower your school librarian to take a leadership role in revitalizing the research process in your school or district?

Chapter 7
Modeling and teaching collaboration

"The world has become far too complex and interrelated for individuals to succeed without collaborative skills"

— James W. Tamm and Ronald J. Luyet

Collaboration is one of those words that is tossed around frequently in schools. Most of us have a general sense of what collaboration means and what it looks like. But it can be difficult to describe exactly what collaboration means as a process.

Let me start by saying that, for me, collaboration is a joyful experience. It means working with others who share common goals, or at least similar goals. It means sharing ideas, taking risks, and creating something together. And it means learning to balance my own needs and interests with the needs and interests of others.

Struggle is involved in one form or another, of course. Working with other people is messy. Let's be real: *humans* are messy. We can be self-centered, absent-minded, lazy, defensive, exhausted, hangry, and worse. But if we're working to build something beautiful together, despite our many imperfections, we often find that not only is the end result worth it, but the effort we put in together was worth it, too. Joy can include struggle.

Earlier in this book, I noted how much I enjoy collaborating with other educators. (Nerdy aside: *enjoy* literally means "to give joy.") This is because a certain kind of energy is created when educators come together to facilitate meaningful learning experiences for students and each other. The ideas I bring to the table are refined and/or expanded, and I learn a ton from what my colleagues bring to the table.

Almost every time, it's my students who benefit the most from my collaborative work. If several adults direct their energy and intellectual resources into a project, that positive energy spreads. Students absorb it. This fact, combined with the actual project that we're working together to facilitate for them, creates an ideal educational experience.

The thing is, 21st century schools need educators who step out of their silos and work with each other. The problems facing young people and schools today — such as a lack of access (Chapter 2) and a lack of inclusivity (Chapter 3) — require us to pool our knowledge and resources in a collective effort to create positive change. Collaboration is absolutely essential and in many classrooms, departments, schools, and districts it's not happening nearly as much as it should.

Cue your friendly neighborhood school librarian. School librarians are expert collaborators because, well, we have to be. The very nature of our work is collaborative. In *Leading from the Library*, Shannon McClintock Miller and William Bass explain:

> *Collaboration is one of the skills required for literacy in today's world, and librarians are master collaborators. We see it in the co-planning of lessons and sharing of resources that impact what and how students learn. Collaboration is a skill that is honed over time, but it's also a skill that is central to library programs around the world.*[116]

With this sentiment in mind, I'll walk you through some of the ways in which 21st century school librarians model collaboration for our educator peers and teach collaboration skills to our students. These

---

116 McClintock Miller, S. & Bass, W. (2019) *Leading from the Library: Help Your School Community Thrive in the Digital Age*, International Society for Technology in Education

two elements are intertwined. It's difficult to teach collaboration skills without regularly collaborating yourself. Hopefully this chapter will inspire you to begin new and successful collaborations in your classroom, department, school, and/or district.

In the first section, I'll share some crucial elements of good collaboration that are rooted in my own experience and the wisdom of others. Next, I'll explore some of the challenges you'll face when collaborating with your colleagues and teaching collaboration to your students.

I'll also detail a few examples of how I've modeled and taught collaboration in my own work as a school librarian and how other librarians throughout the US have done the same. I'll list some suggested takeaways, as well as pointers on how your school librarian can help you move forward with whatever new collaborations you dream up.

The last section includes some guiding questions for teachers and administrators, with the ultimate goal of creating collaborative relationships among educators and among students. The more we model and teach collaboration in our schools, the more opportunities we give our students to learn to work well with others and find joy in the act of creating something together.

Essential elements of collaboration

In *Collaborative Intelligence*, Dr. Dawna Markova and Angie McArthur note that as a society, we're moving from a "market-share" mindset to a "mind-share" mindset:

> *We are now entering a "mind share" world, no longer just dealing with analytic and procedural problems that require rational solutions. We're being asked to think together in ways that are innovative and relational. People who have never met are being forced to come up with breakthrough solutions to complex problems. We must work and think across continents, cultures, time zones, and temperaments.*[117]

---

117   Markova, D. & McArthur, A. (2015) *Collaborative Intelligence: Thinking With People Who Think Differently*, Spiegel & Grau

I can think of no place where the "mind-share" mindset is more important than our K-12 schools.

As I've mentioned, the focus of this chapter is twofold: first, how we can model collaboration for students and other educators, and second, how we can explicitly teach collaboration. The list of essential elements for effective collaboration that you see below is written mostly with educators in mind, but each element also applies to teaching students how to effectively collaborate with each other.

- **A desire to create something beautiful together.** We can't take this one for granted. For all involved parties, there should be a genuine desire to create something with others. Ideally, a desire to work with others to create something *beautiful*. In other words, the goal of the collaboration — its final product, if you will — should be to make something that's very pleasing to all parties. If everyone begins with this goal and this mindset then there's a good chance that good things will come from it.

- **Time for ideation.** Early on, when you and your collaborators meet to discuss the general idea you have in mind, allow each other to imagine freely. The idea here is that, as collaborators, you give each other space to share what you're dreaming up individually. You brainstorm and build on ideas without shutting each other down or talking about constraints just yet. Dream up, dream big. This is an exciting part of the process and creates the kind of group energy that can sustain a collaboration.

- **Regularly scheduled time to chat.** For longer-term collaborations, you'll need regularly scheduled check-ins to touch base on progress and problems, as well as to discuss and plan general maintenance of your project. A recurring invitation on Google Calendar, or its equivalent, works perfectly (same time every week or fortnight, for example). Every time you meet, as with any well-run meeting, you'll need a clear agenda, someone to keep you all on-task, some space for rapport-building, and to leave with concrete, documented plans for the next steps. If no one takes notes and there's no plan for follow-up, much of what's discussed during the meeting will likely be lost, no matter how much you think you'll remember.

- **Shared goals.** Once you figure out what you're working toward together, all collaborators should be as clear as possible about shared goals. These goals need to be specific. If you're creating some kind of lesson, unit, project, or curriculum for students, these could be learning goals. For other collaborative projects, it might be helpful to think about this as developing a shared *purpose*.

- **Individual goals.** In addition to whatever collective goals you've set as a team, it's helpful to have some individual goals in mind as well. What do you hope to gain from this collaboration? If you're working together on a lesson, unit, project, or curriculum for students, what goals specific to your educational role do you want to integrate into your collaborative project? It's important to be upfront about your individual goals with your team, and to periodically remind them about what you're hoping to accomplish, too. It might be helpful to create a document that lists your team's shared goals *and* individual goals.

- **Good communication.** Do your very best to create a culture within your team in which all members feel comfortable talking openly and honestly. If people are holding back then you will likely lose opportunities to discover new ideas that could benefit your collaborative project. Try to communicate as much as possible about your project, so that no one is stepping on another's toes or unwittingly trying to do the same thing simultaneously.

- **Ability to hold things lightly.** Collaboration requires us to genuinely care about the work we're doing with our team, but I would venture to say that it also requires us to not take any of it too seriously. This paradoxical truth is important to keep in mind whenever we're working with others. If we hold things lightly — our expectations, for example — then we don't run the risk of making the whole endeavor into more than it should be. And we don't run the risk of tying our self-worth or professional esteem to the project. This isn't to diminish the power and beauty of a good collaboration. It's just to say that if we lighten our grip, keep a sense of humor, and focus on joy, then we're a lot more likely to enjoy the whole experience.

- **Willingness to compromise.** This is closely related to holding things lightly. When we approach collaboration with a lighter grip on our ideas and/or intended outcomes then we're much more likely to be flexible with our teammates. Honestly, this is difficult for me. When I have an idea I'm particularly excited about it, I want to do it and I want to do it my way. But this mindset is toxic to collaboration. Plus, when I'm willing to yield a little, I often find that the other person's modification or approach works out really well and gives me a fresh perspective. I've had this realization countless times toward the end of a collaboration — sometimes long after — and it's one of the elements of collaboration that makes me want to do it again and again. It demonstrates the power of group thinking. I can't move on from this point without noting how, as a country, we seem quite unable to compromise. This is something we must become better at as education professionals, and it's certainly a skill that our students need in order to build a better tomorrow.

- **Lack of defensiveness.** This, too, is related to holding things lightly. We've all had moments during a collaboration when someone says something that triggers us in one way or another and we can barely (or not at all) contain ourselves from defending our own honor. But if we lead with *curiosity* instead of defensiveness, we're much more likely to learn from the conversation and be productive with our teammates: *Can you tell me more about* _____? Just asking a question like this can give us a few seconds to cool off. And we may also learn that the person(s) didn't intend what they said to be received in the way we heard it, thereby preventing an unnecessary verbal tussle. Provided they are not asked passive-aggressively, clarifying questions can move the conversation forward and avoid a shutdown.

- **Avoidance of tokenism.** This element is mostly for larger, longer-term collaborations, but it's important to keep in mind for any kind of teamwork. In *Collaboration: What Makes it Work*, Dr. Paul W. Mattessich and Kirsten M. Johnson define tokenism as "the practice of making only a perfunctory or symbolic effort toward representation, especially by recruiting a small number of people from underrepresented groups in order to give the appearance of equality."[118] The authors write that to avoid doing this, we must first work to establish connections with diverse individuals and/or organizations. Then, once the collaborating team is established, norms should be developed as a group, as well as possible ways to "integrate different perspectives to inform its decision-making beyond adding individuals … as collaborative members."[119]

Taken together, the elements listed above describe what an effective collaboration looks and feels like. The more we incorporate these elements into our collaborative work, the closer we get to establishing the "mind-share" mindset that we — and the young people we teach — desperately need in order to solve problems at the local, national, and global levels.

Overcoming challenges

As powerful as collaborations can be in schools, they don't happen often enough. There are numerous challenges that prevent them from being started or sustained. In this section I'll share some of these challenges, as well as suggestions for overcoming them. The first list of collaboration-related challenges focuses on those faced frequently by educators; the second list addresses those faced frequently by students.

To be clear: these challenges *must* be overcome. Our students, schools, and communities need us to work together.

Teachers:
- **Lack of time.** The perennial problem for educators: so much to do, so little time. It's certainly on school leaders/administrators to build time for educators to collaborate. This is no small point:

---

118 Mattessich, P.W. & Johnson, K.M. (2018) *Collaboration: What Makes It Work (third edition)*, Fieldstone Alliance
119 Ibid.

school leaders love to hear about and spotlight collaboration, but they don't always make sure all educators have the time in their schedules or during meetings to make it happen. That said, it's also on educators to find or make time to collaborate. This is partially why I began this chapter with the focus on *joy*. If we're genuinely excited about an idea for a collaboration, chances are we'll find or make the time for it to happen. It all starts with sharing an idea with at least one colleague you'd like to work with. Or perhaps connecting with educators at other schools or people outside the education world. Once all parties are interested and committed, you'll just need to compare calendars and commit to regularly scheduled in-person or virtual meetings. Get these meetings on the calendar early and, when they happen, respect everyone's time by ending on time.

- **Culture of silos.** At a few points in this book I've discussed how K-12 educators are mostly siloed. This is more true at some schools than it is at others. If your school culture is one in which pretty much all educators in the building stay in their designated spaces and do their own thing, it can feel strange to be the one to try something new and initiate a collaboration. But don't lose heart. You can be the trailblazer. What begins as (necessarily) countercultural can one day become the norm. Changing your school's culture for the better — and building a more collaborative educational environment absolutely does this — is a crucial form of educational leadership. We need leaders who bring about more collaboration, because collaboration — especially collaboration across content areas or divisions — can make for more energized educators and, in many cases, more energized students.

- **Unhelpful mindsets.** After collaborations are sparked, certain mindsets can make it difficult for the collaboration to be truly successful. For example, if one or more teammates approach the collaboration with lots of rigid, non-negotiable requirements then the team's time together will not be a true collaboration. Mindsets that are focused on the self and/or rigid expectations are non-starters. Instead, we can seek inspiration from design thinking (see Chapter 1), a process in which collaboration is a key tenet. In an article for *Inc.*, Michael Graber points to the "radical" collaboration of design thinking, with the "radical" part suggesting "that we all work in multidisciplinary teams and that we explore ideas, insights, and concepts fearlessly as *equal* team members."[120] It's this kind of open, democratic approach to working together that is necessary for a collaboration to reach its full potential.

- **Personal and/or professional insecurity.** Many educators avoid collaborations because of some kind of insecurity. For example, if you don't ever teach outside your designated teaching space, it can feel pretty uncomfortable to co-teach with colleagues, regardless of whether the co-teaching is happening inside or outside your classroom. Perhaps there's a fear of judgment and/or a lack of confidence. I definitely experienced some of this when I became a school librarian after many years of being fairly siloed as a middle school English teacher. In my own classroom I was confident in my teaching and the way I interacted with students, but when I started working more regularly with different grade levels — especially early elementary students and teachers — I regularly felt uncomfortable. However, it's *good* to step out of our comfort zone, especially in the service of a good collaboration. There's a sense of newness involved in pushing through our insecurities, and whenever there's a sense of newness there are more opportunities for creativity, because we tend to see things in a different light. You can be honest with your colleagues — and with your students — about how the whole experience is new for you and that you're learning, too. That's pretty good modeling right there.

Students:
- **Excessive focus on the final product.** Sometimes the message we give our students at the beginning of a group assignment or project, intentionally or unintentionally, is that the whole

---

120 Graber, M. (2017) "How mindset is greater than process, every time," *Inc.*, www.inc.com/michael-graber/radical-collaboration-mindset-over-process.html

point of working together is the final product. I've been just as guilty as anyone in this regard, particularly when I haven't put as much thought as I should into planning a group assignment or project. It's on us as educators to make sure we communicate to our students that the time they spend collaborating with each other — the challenging collaborative work itself — is just as important, if not *more* important, than their final product. After all, in the long-term, helping our students develop a greater capacity for effective collaboration is far more significant than whatever they produce for our class or school.

- **Lack of time.** Time can be an issue for students, too — often because they're not given enough of it to *really* work together. The first step is to make sure you've allotted sufficient time for real collaborative work to happen. Then you might consider following one of the frameworks for hands-on learning that addresses real-world problems discussed in Chapter 1 (project-based learning, inquiry-based learning, or design thinking). Frameworks such as these can maximize efficiency and therefore help your students make the best use of the time you've given them to collaborate with each other. If you're not following frameworks then requiring students to democratically assign specific roles and establish norms as a group can be helpful on the front end of any collaboration. With enough time to actually do the work, and with some structure and clear expectations in place, students can more successfully enter into a collaboration.

- **Inexperience.** Many students are expected to work effectively and efficiently in groups without ever having received direct instruction in how to collaborate. If "radical collaboration" can be challenging for educators, consider how much more so for our students. We must create opportunities for educators to talk to each other about how they teach collaborative skills, so that first and foremost we know these skills are being taught — but also so we can be intentional about giving students opportunities to practice them over and over again. After all, collaborative skills are not only important in school and in the workplace, but they're also essential for healthy relationships in general.

- **Lack of explicit teaching.** This is certainly related to inexperience, but its importance is such that I want to address it separately. Educators often assign "group work" without considering students' need for collaborative skills to be taught explicitly. This is without doubt a major challenge faced by our students when it comes to collaboration. When we ask students to work together for more than just a few minutes, we need to name the specific skills they will practice. For example, students need us to talk with them about how to actively listen, effectively brainstorm, assign roles, find compromises, and utilize each other's strengths. You could also think about your last collaboration and what part was most difficult for you, then share with your students how you worked through it (or how you wish you had worked through it). Given my emphasis on joy, I also highly recommend doing everything you can to create conditions in which your students can collaborate on projects they're all pretty excited about. (See Chapter 6 for more on this, specifically through the lens of research projects.)

School libraries leading the way

As I noted earlier, I've found collaboration to be immensely satisfying on a personal and professional level. Collaboration has allowed me to build new connections with my colleagues and students, and to deepen connections that already exist.

In *Interactions: Collaboration Skills for School Professionals*, Marilyn Friend and Lynne Cook explain that successful collaborations indeed lead to a stronger sense of community: "In collaboration, participants know that their strengths can be maximized, their weaknesses can be minimized, and the result will be better for all."[121] Because I serve all students and all faculty members in my role as school librarian, I try to model collaboration as often as possible. It's my responsibility to do so. It's also a joy.

Modeling begins by actually *participating* in a variety of collaborations on a regular basis. In Chapter 4, I detailed how I co-facilitate a class

---

121 Friend, M. & Cook, L. (2016) *Interactions: Collaboration Skills for School Professionals* (eighth edition), Pearson

that we currently call "library and technology integration." One of the most important elements of that class is regular time for all the involved educators, including myself, to collaborate with each other. The idea is to plan the next steps and delegate responsibilities for the class that we essentially co-teach together. We keep these meetings short (usually 20-30 minutes) and regular (every week or two), and fill in any gaps via email.

I make a point to join different department/division meetings from time to time to pitch a book or collaboration, or just to learn what's happening in their curriculum and ask how the library could better support them. In terms of sparking new collaborations, I've found it's just as important to be a "go-getter" as it is to actively listen to what's going on in a variety of classrooms.

Another way I seek to model collaboration is to share, in one form or another, the results of the collaborative teaching and learning experiences in which I have participated. For example, when my school transitioned to virtual learning at the beginning of the Covid-19 pandemic, a colleague and I wanted to make sure our students' projects could not only continue, but could still be shared with the community — as in the original plan. We were unable to have students put together an in-person exhibit, so we worked with them to create a virtual museum.

Despite the challenging circumstances, we felt it was crucial to co-create with our students a venue where they could share their work with others in our community. I consider this sharing to be an important form of modeling and even advocacy. When collaborative teaching and/or learning projects are shared regularly within a school, other educators see the great things that can come from them. Consistent sharing and modeling goes a long way toward drumming up interest in and support for more collaboration.

I regularly serve on search committees for new faculty members, and I've found that facilitating collaborative exercises with finalist candidates can be an incredibly useful way to gauge their interest in and comfort with collaboration. During these collaborative exercises, which generally run for about 30 minutes, we have an informal brainstorming session with them about an area of their expertise, during which we talk about how we could build a cross-curricular lesson or project together. The idea is to give us a good sense of their collaborative skills and the candidate a sense of what it's like to collaborate with their would-be colleagues.

Another way I try to model collaboration at my school is by positioning the school library itself as a welcoming and essential collaborative workspace. This has required some advocacy on my part, such as convincing our middle school division head to move collaborative study halls for sixth, seventh, and eighth graders to the library. I also facilitate a student-staffed writing center in which students help their peers, and encourage faculty to choose the library for anything from small department meetings to meetings for entire divisions. Each of these decisions is discussed in more detail in Chapter 2, but I bring them up again here because they've really helped our school community see the library as a collaborative workspace for students and faculty — a space where knowledge is co-created, not just found or taught.

As often as possible, I teach collaboration skills in context. I try not to assign group projects just for the sake of it. If I'm asking students to work together, I want to make sure the conditions are right for them to do so. For example, students must have adequate scaffolding in terms of collaboration skills, described earlier in this chapter as the *essential elements of collaboration*. When facilitating collaborative student projects, I alternate between teaching certain skills up front, such as how to actively listen, and teaching others at the beginning of future stages of the process. Trying to front-load the teaching of all collaborative skills just isn't effective. There's no way students will remember everything, and learning about those skills isn't as meaningful when they're not tied directly to something they're currently working through.

If I'm asking students to work together on something, the work itself needs to be multifaceted. In an article for *Edutopia*, Mary Burns discusses this very important element of student collaboration:

> *If the assignment is too simple, they can more easily do it alone. At most, they may check in with each other or interact in superficial ways. The real reason to collaborate is because the task is complex — it is too difficult and has too many pieces to complete alone. ...*

One way to do this is through rigorous projects that require students to identify a problem (for example, balancing population growth in their city with protection of existing green spaces) and agree — through research, discussion, debate, and time to develop their ideas — on a solution which they must then propose together.[122]

The inquiry-based approach to teaching and learning that Burns advocates is outlined in more detail in Chapter 1. I can't recommend enough this approach — and the others described in Chapter 1 — for guiding students toward and through truly meaningful collaborative learning experiences.

When teaching collaboration skills, I'm most successful whenever I'm as clear as possible with students about what a certain collaboration skill looks and sounds like. When these skills are reinforced time and time again, students really do begin to develop a collaborative mindset that allows them to delight in new challenges and work with their peers to explore — and even create — possible solutions.

Forward-thinking librarians

Len Bryan, school librarian at Spring Woods High School in Houston, Texas, begins collaborating with faculty before the school year even starts. "I volunteered to teach new teachers how to use the online gradebook, learning management system, attendance trackers, and the other tools they needed to do their jobs," he tells me. "While I had them together, I'd also teach them how to schedule time in the library and about the types of resources we had available, along with ideas for using them in their grade levels and/or subject areas." These conversations and lessons inevitably led to future collaborations.

Bryan does everything he can to enter into conversations with teachers about curriculum, from joining meetings when teachers are comfortable with him doing so to casually sharing resources that might be helpful. "My strategies have ranged from curating resources and sharing them with teachers, to on-demand research instruction, to full-class or even grade-

---

122   Burns, M. (2016) "5 strategies to deepen student collaboration," *Edutopia*,
      www.edutopia.org/article/5-strategies-deepen-student-collaboration-mary-burns

level takeovers, to teaching entire inquiry units over the course of several weeks," Bryan says. He has also been willing to take the lead on long-term units. "I once taught all sections of 11th grade AP American history in our lecture hall — 90-120 students at a time — four periods per day, for two weeks. Their research projects, which were videos with transcripts, were assessed using rubrics I helped the teachers create, and I graded their bibliographies while teachers focused on grading the projects themselves."

It's this kind of flexibility and willingness to dive into big projects whenever possible that enables school librarians like Bryan to become expert collaborators. Bryan believes that modeling collaboration, combined with explicitly teaching collaboration skills, is the best way to teach collaboration to students — and the best way to create an overall culture of collaboration in a school. "A culture of collaboration is a must-have, as too often students are thrown together in groups without proper training," Bryan tells me. "This can lead to one or two conscientious students doing all the work while others coast, or complete group breakdown, *Lord of the Flies*-style."

For Bryan, collaboration between librarians and teachers is essential to teach students 21st century library skills, including collaboration and multiple literacies. "Library and information literacy skills taught in isolation and not immediately applied to real academic work are soon forgotten," he explains. "We do our best work when we do it alongside teachers, modeling what respectful communication, conflict resolution, time and materials management, and taking responsibility look like for our students in real-time. When authentic collaboration is part of the school culture, students win by getting a much richer educational experience, and teachers win by gaining a true instructional partner. Many hands make light work!"

Amanda Jones, school librarian at Live Oak Middle School in Watson, Louisiana, is one of *School Library Journal*'s two School Librarians of the Year 2021. Like Bryan, Jones starts the year by planting the seeds of future collaborations. "At the beginning of the year, I give teachers a list of open dates for the library for the fall, and I send out an email with a Google Form where they can choose a few dates to book," Jones explains. "Then, about two weeks before it's time for their library date, I email them and ask them what skills and standards they will be covering around that time. I ask them if they have any idea of what they would like to cover during the library time or if they would like me to start off the collaboration. They usually want me to start it off, so after they give me a list of what they want to cover, I send some ideas."

As one might expect from a School Librarian of the Year, Jones has all sorts of tools in her toolbox. "I might suggest using their public library student eCards to do research on the topic, a breakout box or digital escape room, a virtual trip, or I might give them some ideas for tech tools, such as Flipgrid, green-screen activities, stop-motion animation, and augmented reality activities. After I give them some suggestions, we email back and forth until we come up with a formal plan. On the day of their visit, I make sure I have all the teaching materials ready, and the teacher and I will often co-teach the lesson together."

One of Jones' specific collaborations revolved around a fifth-grade English language arts class reading *Flipped* by Wendelin Van Draanen. Jones had read the book and she had an idea. "I remembered that at the beginning, one of the characters raises chickens and there's an incident with chicken eggs," she explains. She saw an opportunity to do some hands-on research with students, using the plot of the book as a springboard.

"I asked the teacher if she would be interested in getting an incubator and some eggs, and we could have the students come in on their library day for research on what happens during the incubation period. She was on board, and so we created a design thinking challenge in which students created a chicken coop after doing some research, and then we live-streamed the eggs hatching on our library website the next week."

Clearly, Jones is invested in designing authentic collaborative learning experiences for her students. She is also invested in teaching specific collaboration skills, which she acknowledges can be difficult at times with her middle school students. Just as with initiating teaching collaborations, Jones begins teaching collaborative skills at the beginning of the year.

"Most of my library lessons involve group work of some kind at some point," she tells me. "At the beginning of the year, I teach a mini-lesson on collaboration during students' orientation visit to the library. We have an open discussion about the importance of being respectful, and they express what tends to bother them the most about collaboration. Then I turn the conversation around to have them visualize and describe their best-case scenarios when working with partners. After this, I have them write something positive about their partners, and they all read these positive notes to each other. I remind them of the lesson every single time every class comes to the library for the rest of the year."

Going back to modeling, Jones says she feels strongly that educators share the results of collaborations with their larger school community and their district. "I want students to see that I will work with all their teachers to create exciting lessons," she explains. "I want the parents and community to see that school librarians do more than just check out books. I want the district to see that school librarians are essential."

One of her primary goals is to help students learn how to work well with each other. "And since I teach every student in the school," Jones says, "who better to help them work on their collaboration skills than me?"

Takeaways for all educators

Educators across grade levels and subject areas can model and teach collaboration. Because modeling and teaching are interrelated, it's important to prioritize both. Each has the ability to impact your comfort and skill with the other.

If you're a teacher who's looking to initiate new collaborations with colleagues and also be more intentional about teaching collaboration skills to your students, I recommend first taking a few minutes to jot down any ideas that have been floating around in your mind for a while and/or any new ideas that have come up while reading this chapter.

Consider how and when you and your students might benefit the most from collaborations. Once you have a few specific options in mind, you can discern which are most exciting and/or important to you personally and professionally, and then connect with colleagues who might be interested in partnering with you or willing to offer ideas about how to teach collaboration skills in context to your students. Or perhaps you'll find the ability to do both at the same time, such as through a teaching collaboration centered around a project-based learning unit.

You might also consider reflecting on which of the essential elements of collaboration, outlined earlier in this chapter, you have worked on with your students. Within each of those elements are specific skills. For example, active listening is an important part of good communication. You could spend a little time identifying exactly which skills you have taught already, which skills could be reinforced, and which you haven't taught at all.

If you find yourself siloed in your role and/or in your classroom, consider how you might establish your teaching space as a collaborative space. From bringing in expert guests to co-teaching lessons or units with colleagues, there are plenty of options for bringing other voices into the space. You don't have to do this all the time, and these collaborations can be short and sweet. It's important to keep in mind that, regardless of their length and frequency, teaching collaborations bring with them a special kind of energy that can help you expand the scope of your class(es). They also help you practice what you preach about collaborative skills.

And don't forget to share your collaborations after they occur: with your colleagues, with parents, with other students, with your district, and/or on personal or school social media accounts. In schools where educators are mostly siloed, sharing your collaborative experiences — as well as the collaborative experiences of your students — can go a long way toward building a "mind-share" mindset in your school.

Administrators, I cannot stress enough the importance of leading your school toward a more collaborative culture — one in which you model collaboration yourself, highlight collaborative teaching partnerships by passing the mic to those teachers, and celebrate student collaborations as often and as widely as possible. Giving airtime to those who have participated in successful collaborations is a way of honoring this work and allowing teachers and students to develop their own leadership skills.

As an administrative leader, modeling collaboration really does begin with you. One of the most important ways to do this is to host democratic meetings about important topics as often as possible — meetings in which you're there as just another participant, not the person leading the charge. This means moving from a "power over" frame of mind, in which you exercise power through control over others, to a "power with" framework, which is based on mutual respect and shared influence.[123]

I've attended numerous meetings with administrators in which they've taken this approach and, when it's done well, it makes all the difference in the world. You may have the final say about certain topics and issues, but if you model effective collaboration skills then the educators you work with will take notice. This is, of course, an important form of teaching.

How your school librarian can help

As expert collaborators, school librarians are poised and ready to help you model and teach collaboration. Teachers, if you're inspired to initiate a new collaboration with your school librarian, first consider what level of collaboration would work best for you. In *The Many Faces of School Library Leadership*, Anthony Tilke summarizes the four facets of collaboration between teachers and the school librarian, as identified by Patricia Montiel-Overall in her study "Toward a theory of collaboration for teachers and librarians."[124]

- "**Coordination**, where both librarian and teacher are aware of each other's activities in a given curriculum area, and so this level of collaboration is more focused on communication."

- "**Cooperation**, where both teacher and librarian work on a project or unit, with each maintaining their own specialized functions."

- "**Integrated instruction**. Here both librarian and teacher work together in an environment of 'interest,' 'commitment,' and 'trust.'"

- "**Integrated curriculum**. Here librarians and teachers work together in an environment where such collaboration is the norm. Indeed, the role of the principal is important in this level of collaboration, not least in providing resources and time."[125]

123 https://brenebrown.com/wp-content/uploads/2020/10/Brene-Brown-on-Power-and-Leadership-10-26-20.pdf

124 Montiel-Overall, P. (2005) "Toward a theory of collaboration for teachers and librarians," American Association of School Librarians, https://files.eric.ed.gov/fulltext/EJ965627.pdf

125 Tilke, A. (2017) "The teacher librarian as curriculum and instructional practitioner and leader," in Coatney, S. & Harada, V. *The Many Faces of School Library Leadership* (second edition), Libraries Unlimited

In any of these different levels or facets of teaching collaborations, school librarians can also help you explicitly teach collaboration skills through lessons that involve group work in one form or another. Because your students are our students, too, we care deeply that they learn to work well with each other.

If you're looking for "coordination," you could let us know about an important lesson, unit, or project coming up for students that will rely heavily upon students collaborating effectively with each other. We will do everything we can to make sure we deliver the specific collaboration skills that you're hoping we can teach and/or review. Teaching these skills is more difficult to do out of context, so we'll likely deliver them through some kind of short collaborative activity and group reflection.

If you're looking for "cooperation," we can work together to teach collaboration skills to your students. We can be most effective (read: most prepared) to work with you if you give us as much notice as possible about your proposed collaboration. I regularly collaborate with teachers in this way, and it often involves co-teaching to some degree. I show up to teach 21st century library skills (among them collaboration skills), usually by building on something that's already happening in that class's curriculum. Because teachers are in the same space, they learn more about these skills and new or different approaches to teaching them.

"Integrated instruction" is a bit more involved and in my experience is often an evolution of "cooperation." Because deeper levels of mutual trust have been established, the teacher(s) and librarian find themselves engaging students in such a way that the lines blur between their different roles. When this level of collaboration occurs, students extend questions equally to teacher(s) and librarian, and both educators are equally prepared to address their questions.

"Integrated curriculum," in which 21st century school library skills are successfully integrated into a teacher's curriculum and a longer-term partnership is created, involves a lot of planning time for the educators. But whenever and wherever integrated curriculum is achieved, the mind-share mindset between the teacher(s) and librarian is in full effect. This usually means that the curriculum has more breadth and depth than it would otherwise. As such, students participate in a superior learning experience.

Administrators, we can help you in your efforts to model and teach collaboration to faculty and students. If provided with a forum to do so, we can share successful collaborative teaching experiences with faculty and then offer all of them this same service. If you don't already, encourage your school librarian to serve on hiring committees for new faculty members and ask questions about their experience of teaching collaborations. Or, ideally, ask us to facilitate real-time collaborative exercises with finalists. We can help you determine which candidates have the collaborative spirit you're looking for.

If you'd like to move your school or district in the direction of more integrated instruction and integrated curriculum, you'll need to empower your school librarian(s) through "resources and time," as noted by Montiel-Overall in her study.[126] This will obviously look different from school to school and district to district, but the important part is that we are set up for success when it comes to being able to further integrate into classrooms. As I've noted numerous times in this book, our reach extends to all students and all teachers in the school. Once empowered, school librarians can begin making positive systemic change — one collaboration at a time.

Better together

The "mind-share" culture that develops in schools through collaborations between educators has the ability to make teaching and learning deeper and more enjoyable for educators and students alike. Problems become more easily solved and inspiration more freely shared.

When we regularly give students opportunities to collaborate, while being clear with them about what collaboration skills are and how to use them effectively, we gift them the ability to create "mind-share" cultures of their own one day. After all, if there's anything our world needs right now, it's for people to be able to work together.

---

126 Montiel-Overall, P. (2005) "Toward a theory of collaboration for teachers and librarians," American Association of School Librarians, https://files.eric.ed.gov/fulltext/EJ965627.pdf

With this in mind, below are two sets of guiding questions: one for teachers and one for administrators. It's my hope that these questions will inspire you to take a few steps today toward more modeling and more teaching of collaboration.

Teachers:
- Think of one successful collaboration of which you've been a part, as an educator or otherwise. What are some of the elements that made it successful?
- What are a couple of new ways you could model collaboration skills for your students? Are there any educators with whom you want to collaborate?
- Which collaboration skills do you already teach? How could you teach them more effectively?
- Which collaboration skills do you not explicitly teach? Where and how could you teach them? How can your school librarian help?

Administrators:
- What are a few specific ways you could more intentionally exercise "power with" (see page 189)? How would doing so lead to a stronger culture of collaboration in your school or district?
- How often do you celebrate faculty collaborations? How often do you celebrate student collaborations? Where and how could you publicly celebrate both more often?
- Are you quite intentional about seeking new faculty members who possess demonstrable collaborative skills? What are some steps you could take to become more intentional about this?
- Have you equipped your school librarian(s) with all the resources and time they need to create a culture of collaboration? If not, what could you do today to better equip them?

Afterword

This book was written in the midst of the Covid-19 pandemic. It feels important to mention this here for two primary reasons.

First, taking on a long-form writing project proved to be a great way to focus — meditate, even — on something positive each day. Something that wasn't related to sickness, isolation, and all the other awful things we've had to worry about since the pandemic started. I'm grateful to have had this opportunity.

Second, my school library, like many others, was physically closed for the 2020-21 school year. There was this strange new distance between me and the otherwise familiar topics and experiences I was writing about. I was able to — forced to — write in a more reflective manner. I had more of a bird's-eye view, more of a critical eye, than I might have if our library had been fully open. A silver lining to the closure, perhaps.

That said, even if this book had been written under more "normal" circumstances, I would have been just as humbled by the amazing work that school librarians have done and continue to do every day. Each librarian interviewed for this book is an inspiration, and they are just a few of the tens of thousands of school librarians in the US. I learned a ton from those I spoke to and those I read about, so it's not surprising that I found myself making changes to my own programming, curricula, and overall view of school librarianship as I wrote the book. I feel renewed.

However, I'd be lying if I said that I didn't occasionally feel overwhelmed, too, by the sheer number of tasks for which 21st century school libraries are responsible. And given the fact that this book asks teachers and administrators to adopt key focus areas of school librarianship, I recognize the hugeness of this call to action. As educators, we're already asked to do a lot. But this is because we have one of the most important jobs in the world: caring for and teaching young people. By working together, we can absolutely make significant progress in each of the focus areas laid out in this book.

The best advice I have to give on this front — because it has worked for me — comes from the author and speaker Rob Bell, who writes: "You throw yourself into it, and you hold it loosely."[127] The answer to moving forward, I think, is in this paradox.

The work of being an educator is endlessly dynamic and baffling, energizing and exhausting. We can't do it all every day, but each day we can give it our all. And while we work we can do our very best to not stress about outcomes. There's a lot that is out of our control, anyway.

May we all do our best to throw ourselves into this work of caring for and teaching young people, and at the same time hold it loosely. It's in this balance that we can be our best selves and encourage our students to do the same.

---

127   Bell, R. (2020) *Everything is Spiritual: Who We Are and What We're Doing Here,* St Martin's Essentials

Acknowledgements

Katie Tahmaseb, for always encouraging my work in education, especially in those moments when I have felt anxious and discouraged.

Mark Combes at John Catt Educational, for believing in this book — and me — from the beginning.

Isla McMillan at John Catt Educational, for her expert editing and kind support.

Joel Smith, for his help early in the process of mapping out this book, and also for his help with countless pieces of writing over the years.

Jenna Chandler-Ward, for her guidance on Chapter 3 while she was working on her own book.

All the librarians and library-adjacent educators who generously took the time to talk to me — during a pandemic — about what they do and how they do it. This is your book, too.

All my colleagues at the Meadowbrook School of Weston, many of whom are like family, for inspiring me to be my best each day.

All my students over the years, for their contagious energy and passion for learning. I started taking my own writing seriously because of you all, and you've pushed me to be the best educator I can be.

And to my own kids, Noah and Grace, for helping me imagine a better future.